C000017322

LITERARY EXPLORATIONS

CONTEMPORARY FICTION AND POETRY

DR. ABHIMANYU PANDEY

ANAPHORA LITERARY PRESS

QUANAH, TEXAS

ANAPHORA LITERARY PRESS
1108 W 3rd Street
Quanah, TX 79252
https://anaphoraliterary.com

Book design by Anna Faktorovich, Ph.D.

Copyright © 2019 by Abhimanyu Pandey

All rights reserved. No part of this book may be reproduced in any form or by any electronic or mechanical means, including information storage and retrieval systems, without permission in writing from Abhimanyu Pandey. Writers are welcome to quote brief passages in their critical studies, as American copyright law dictates.

Printed in the United States of America, United Kingdom and in Australia on acid-free paper.

Cover Images: Michael Ondaatje speaks for the Tulane Great Writer Series presented by the Creative Writing Fund of the Department of English. Dixon Hall; October 25, 2010.
Khaled Hosseini in 2007. White House photo by David Bohrer.
Margaret Atwood at the 2017 Frankfurt Book Fair.
Sylvia Plath in July 1961 at her Chalcot Square flat in London.

Published in 2019 by Anaphora Literary Press

Literary Explorations: Contemporary Fiction and Poetry
Abhimanyu Pandey—1st edition.

Library of Congress Control Number: 2019906457
Library Cataloging Information
Pandey, Abhimanyu, 1992-, author.
   Literary explorations: Contemporary fiction and poetry / Abhimanyu
   Pandey
   106 p. ; 9 in.
   ISBN 978-1-68114-505-1 (softcover : alk. paper)
   ISBN 978-1-68114-506-8 (hardcover : alk. paper)
   ISBN 978-1-68114-507-5 (e-book)
1. Literary Criticism—Poetry. 2. Literary Criticism—Comparative Literature.
3. Literary Criticism—Modern—General.
PN172-239: Literature: Authorship: Technique. Literary Composition
809: Literature History, Description & Criticism

CONTENTS

Preface   5

Evolution in Magical Realism: American and Indian   6

The Question of Voice and Sylvia Plath   28

The Postmodern Hero in *The English Patient* and   36
    Londonstani

Showcasing Masculinity: *The Kite Runner*   45

Narrative Skills, Language and Dialogue in Gautam   66
    Malkani's *Londonstani*

Culture, Language and the Post-Truth World   89

The Biographical and Autobiographical: Two Canadian   96
    Poems

PREFACE

The articles in this volume were written between 2014 and 2018. Some of them sprang out of my thesis on Contemporary Multicultural Fiction while others were either unconnected with it. Some of them resulted from the desire to write on topics that had no connection my doctoral dissertation.

The period in which these articles were written was one of intensive study and research. I have never written so much in my life, and writing means studying with fervor. I will never forget this period because it was that hallowed time in which my mind was beginning to acquire maturity and the student in me was taking a concrete shape. It was a time when I was so steeped in the pleasures of scholarship and research that I often often lost track of time. It was a time that changed the direction of my life from an aimless wanderer to one who had a clear road to be taken.

I am grateful to the teachers of the Department of English & MEL, University of Allahabad, particularly to my mentor Prof. L R Sharma, from whom I learned so much during this period and the period just preceding it. I am especially indebted to the library staff of the University of Allahabad Library and the library of the Central University of Kerala without whose help I would be at sea while trying to collect my material. I cannot forget the discussions I had with some fellow researchers of my wonderful Department. Discussions led to debates and debates brought forth more ideas.

The atmosphere and the architecture of the Department of English of the Allahabad University are unique and unparalleled. They make one either creative or critical. Of course, there is creativity even in being critical and being creative also involves the critical faculty. I found myself drifting towards critical explorations and this book gradually became a living reality.

CHAPTER ONE

Evolution in Magical Realism:
American and Indian

agical Realism has appeared in different forms, recently, accepting something from the author's nationality but also transcending it. Scholars in the West have felt that due to the number of differently styled versions of magical realism the term has begun to signal a hodgepodge. However, Homi K. Bhabha believes that "'Magical realism' after the Latin American Boom, becomes the literary language of the emergent post-colonial world."[1] Nonetheless, with the coming of age of postmodern writing, magical realism seems to have acquired a more global form; gradually diminishing East-West boundaries. Its discourse does not only include "a kind of international literary diaspora" but a "fictional cosmopolitanism" (Wendy B. Faris, 101), it becomes postmodern in a positive sense. But then, scholars have tended to consider it inferior to the best forms of literary writing; escapist, debased, confused, irresponsible, and even wanting. Though some of the best Western minds deliberating on postmodernism, such as the intellectual opponents, Fredric Jameson and Linda Hutcheon, have written about magical realism; they have accepted it with reservations. But, magical realism has proved itself rather flexible and absorbing in its recent avatars. If T. S. Eliot had thought of magical realism when he placed himself on the side of classicism in 1928 (the German term Magischer Realismus was first used in 1925), he might have written "Tradition and the Individual Talent" differently. He limited himself by speaking of only Western authors, Homer down. The romantic imagination, as contained in magical realism, has reached beyond the merely classicist, or the merely occidental; it seems to have brought together the purviews of the Orient and the Occident.

This article is *not* a comprehensive account on the nature or history of magical realism. It attempts to do two things: (i) It shows how mystical and extra-rational elements (like accepting the principle of rebirth) that inform magical realism have often been associated with the colonized, sometimes of the East, but which nonetheless due to hybridization have entered the fiction of the West as well recently. Gabriel García Márquez employed the magical realist style to articulate the "surreal" aspects of postcolonial reality in South America. But now an American novelist, Robin Gregory (2015), has gone beyond the surreal, into the realms of more South Asian and Eastern modes of spiritual understanding. She has added to an American magical tale, perspectives that seem to be rather Indian and of the Far East. (ii) How a recent Indian magical realist novel, Lakshmi Raj Sharma's *The Tailor's Needle* (2009), is able to assimilate into its Eastern flavour a more Western mode of expression via its multiculturalism. From the above two premises it might be concluded that in its recent forms, in the last ten years or so, magical realism has been helping fiction to become more hybrid, taking in much from the East and the West. It is making more plausible the process that Homi K. Bhabha has visualized as "hybridization". In this form magical realism can embrace the nature of fairytales which wipe out East and West and end up as human tales. Novels like *The Improbable Wonders of Moojie Littleman* and *The Tailor's Needle* that have their roots in fairytale-structures, manage to wipe out their East or West, national or regional, character to become more global tales. Like Shakespeare's works, they reflect human nature instead of particular societies. A fairytale can and often does have the potential to accommodate all humanity. It can lay down the foundational structure on which an enduring classic can be constructed. Society often pulls the mind towards an unpleasant reality; human nature and imagination can portray and picture magical possibility.

Even Edward Said had considered the Orient not as something that is fixed and incapable of reaching out to the West:

> ...[T]he Orient is not an inert fact of nature. It is not merely *there*, just as the Occident itself is not just *there* either. We must take Vico's great observation that men make their own history, that what they can know is what they have made, and extend it to geography: as both geographical and cultural entities... The two geographical entities thus support and to an extent reflect each other. (*Orientalism* 4-5)

Bhabha gives to this same postulate a more binding conceptualization when he approvingly states the view of Gyan Prakash in *The Location of Culture*:

> It is difficult to overlook the fact that… third world voices… speak within and to discourses familiar to the 'West'… The Third World, far from being confined to its assigned space, has penetrated the inner sanctum of the 'First World' in the process of being 'Third Worlded'—arousing, inciting and affiliating with the subordinated others in the First World… to connect with minority voices. (354)

Robin Gregory's novel, though young adult fiction, can be read as a fairytale as well as an adult novel. It takes much from several versions of the genre of magical realism and adds to it an Indian or Eastern point of view along with thoughts that are usually associated with William Wordsworth's poetry. Before Gregory, when one thought of magical realism, one generally thought of prose-fiction, but she has added thoughts that are ingrained in Wordsworth's poetry. With her novel it becomes evident that the seeds of magical realism can be found in poets and poet-dramatists long before prose adopted it as an art form. William Shakespeare used it and Wordsworth's romantic forays, in particular, can be seen to encapsulate much that has been associated with magical realism as it is found in Gregory's novel. The title of Gregory's novel, containing the words, "improbable" and "wonders" has a hint of the magical realism it is to encompass—*The Improbable Wonders of Moojie Littleman*. This novel's distinction lies not only in the fact that it has won so many awards (https://robingregory.net/awards-nominations/) but that it has used magical realism in a very distinctive manner. Her magical realism combines a little of some earlier forms of this literary genre but it has moved away from them. Gregory replied to me in an interview with her, dated Feb. 2, 2017 maintaining that she read *Hundred Years of Solitude* about ten times. But for some reason, the anxiety of influence could be one, she has very little of Gabriel García Márquez in her novel. It contains marked similarities with Indian and other spiritual content from the East and it enters into the modes of Wordsworthian thought to be discussed later in this article.

I

There are several varieties of magical realism and Gregory's version is a clear advancement in the genre's evolution. It is not an admixture of dream and reality even though dreams do play a role in it. Nor is it a simple fusion of reality and fantasy. It is an amalgamation of Eastern (particularly Indian) wisdom with a worldview belonging to the West. In a world where most of its protagonist's, family and friends are conceived as people living in a Western society, Moojie Littleman and the supernatural tribe he encounters think as people in the Orient do. Instead of coming up with a surreal world, the novel shows an encounter between the real and the unreal world. Of the unreal world, only Moojie is able to experience, what Wordsworth would describe as "the unknown modes of being". In both the novels discussed in this article, we are brought to worlds that are moral, with poetic justice, and in them the magical and the real blend flawlessly. In them we do not have the surreal or a world marked by the intense irrationality of a dream, as in Márquez. "In my dreams, I was inventing literature," wrote Márquez describing his experience in writing the novel. (See Paul Elie, Jan. 2016)

In *Moojie Littleman*, we never enter a dream world as we do in *One Hundred Years of Solitude*. In Gregory's novel, a dream is a dream and can even contain the germ of what is to happen, as dreams sometimes indicate future happenings in our lives. But the novel's world does not function like a dream world; it is a moral world in which our actions decide the future we are to have. Instead, a clear bridge is made between the real and the magical and the final impression is that realism is something superficial, conceived with the limited vision of a social perception. People tend to rationalize things in the real world as is suggested in the first paragraph of the novel. People hardly find them wondrous as Moojie is to do:

> He [Moojie] arrived on the heels on an earthquake. A minor hiccup as disasters go, the murmur rippling undersea, causing... spider crabs to flood the beach like a ghostly pink tide. It was the sort of earthquake that hushes everything for an instant before nesting birds and sleeping butterflies burst out of

trees.... It is the sort of earthquake that the nuns... would call a mystical grumble. Really there was nothing about it to suggest the terrible *wonders* looming on the horizon. (1)

Moojie's wonders are not like these; they are improbable. In them the magical is there somewhere, waiting in the wings, ready to connect with the real at any time. We are very much in the real world when we enter the universe of *Moojie Littleman*. There is a clear indication of a historically understood time and geographically understood place. But from these we keep entering places that are difficult to locate geographically or historically; we are always conscious that the magical world is only an extension of the real. We are in the early twentieth century (229), in the American setting of San Miguel. But we are made aware that our past births, that could be ancient, have not left us (154); there continue to be meeting points of our past lives with our present journeys of life. The return from the magical to the real locales is fast and frequent as in fairytales. The unreal mountain, cave, forest, etc., at El Serrat are presented as fairly real even when we are continually told about the miracles, rebirths, or simply magical happenings, within them. Somewhere in the distant spatial reaches as well as in the distant past, there seems to be a connectedness of everything. Moojie, the hero-lad of this novel, who grows into his teens, is crippled due to paralysis. Medical science cannot come to his aid; crutches are all that he has been provided by it. As a result, his treatment that uses "alternative means" (6) is found in unreal worlds and this treatment finally cures the boy's paralysis. We are introduced, through this fiction, to remedies that result from positive and good action. This interestingly, is the backbone reality of *The Tailor's Needle* as well.

Moojie Littleman, the protagonist of this novel, is rather aptly positioned to bridge the gap between realism and magical realism because he is the offspring, in all probability, of a gypsy named Adolf the Green and one of the Light Eaters, Afsoun. The gypsy was a bandit and the marriage couldn't work because of which they left Moojie in a bucket (86):

"Let me tell you the story... fifteen summers ago," she [Ninty] began, "a gypsy came to St. Isidore's, a young man, to be precise, with a gunshot wound to his leg.... Dressed top to bottom in green garments, he called himself Adolf the Green. We took him in—against our better judgment and we healed him. At the time, there was a maiden with us named Afsoun. Despite Adolf's contempt for the colour of our skin, despite his barbarous manner, Afsoun was charmed by the man and ran off with him. Come spring there was a baby, my lord, a boy, which we learned had been left at the village chapel.... I suspect the maiden Afsoun and the bandit were, in point of fact, your first parents." (108)

Moojie is then adopted by Henry and Kate Littleman. He grows to the age of eight and then Kate dies. It was the death of the loving Kate and the desertion by his father, Henry, which probably awakens the magical perceptions of Moojie. The magical world is already there in the background, but Moojie begins his journey into it only after he is left sufficiently alone to have his inner perceptions awakened reminding one of Jack in *Jack and the Beanstalk*.

Robin Gregory is fascinated by the wisdom of the East, for instance, she is drawn to "monks who can sit naked on frozen lakes at the height of winter and thaw with their own heat, icy, water-soaked sheets wrapped around their bodies." (6) Though she never tells in clear terms that these monks are, they seem to be hermits from the East; they could be from Tibet, or, possibly, Indian Hindus in the Himalayas. That we are ultimately firmly linked with each other seems to be the philosophy of this real as well as magical world where every act of "worldlings" (40), or the inhabitants of the earth, is noticed and called to account. Moojie is fascinated by a book his mother reads to him, *The Waltzing Lobster*, a book which takes him into a phase of history when great warriors were born "out of heads" and "auspicious children had their very own planets." (7) We are taken into a world, apparently real, in which a certain kind of wisdom prevails; a wisdom that is knowable only by the supernatural spirits referred to as "Light-Eaters". Members of this clan or tribe can interact with Moojie because he was connected with them in a past life and was even, in this life, born of the union of one parent belonging to this clan (Afsoun). In my interview with her on February 1, 2017 [henceforth to be referred to as Interview], Gregory talks of a book, *The Genius of the Few*, by Christian and Barbara O'Brien. It seems rather evident that this book is a parent text of *Moojie Littleman*. Gregory believes that this book "is a study of the earliest written creation story which is dated 3500 BC. In it, there is a supernatural race of beings that came to Earth to civilize humans. Moojie Littleman is an attempt to bring ancient mysticism to modern life in a fresh, natural way."

Gregory considers America "shameful" with regard to the rights of the aborigines. (Interview) This suggests that her mind is open to other regions apart from her home country, America, and she is secular enough to see other religions and worldviews empathetically. Her sympathy for peoples of every colour and nationality can be seen in the novel (101). Like the *The Genius of the Few*, her novel takes the reader eastward. From this it is evident that she has the inclination to look into the cultures and spiritualties of the East and the Far East. The Light Eaters have come from the Far East (53).

On the one hand, *Moojie* is a treatise on Love. From the beginning till the end we are told about the various faces of love. This novel seems to frequently avoid the Christian sense of love contained in the priest's words:

> Love comes in all stripes," the priest said. There's family love; there's husband-and-wife love, there's parent-and-child love. And there's the love of Our Lord who took the deceased home." He looked at Moojie and Papa. "Ours is not to question why. (16)

But this is not the love that the novel places before the reader as the ideal. The idea of love privileged by the author is the one she constructs from Eastern viewpoints, in addition to what she has understood herself about it, but sometimes in opposition to a Christian conception of love. The novel shows Henry Littleman wanting to escape the act of loving and nurturing his adopted son after his wife is dead. Auntie Tilda makes the prophetic statement: "Children make the grandest teachers, don't they? Talk to them and you learn to listen; listen and you learn to love." (18) It takes the whole novel to make Henry understand this. Moojie, may be Henry's adopted son but he is "the father of the man" in the Wordsworthian sense. He has understood much earlier in life, and in a mature manner, what love is. Moojie has been blessed with the magical, intuitive circumstance that has taught him everything about true love. The magical realism of this novel uses the magical to enlighten the real. Moojie is ahead of every other "worldling" in the novel because he has been blessed with the company of the the

Light-Eaters, the Akil-Nuri supernatural tribe, which makes it possible for him to evolve into true love, the kind of love that connects living beings with their universe and converts lovers into light. The following lines and ideas in this book could further help in seeing how this happens: Moojie gazed out of the window at a "bough of stars. *Love.* It was still a mystery to him.... he was just starting to live." (64) This mystery about true love is no longer a mystery at the end of the novel. Moojie is told by one of the clan (Shar) that, "You are light!" (69) Manish's words further explain this: "Praise the light that makes wind.... Praise the spirit of love! I see your light! All is light!" (69) "Everything is light!" the twins had said and they seemed to have read, though they had actually not, the book *The Waltzing Lobster* which said, "The universe is light." (69) Moojie believed that the twins, Shar and Manish, were saints.

From the above, it is possible to see that love and light are synonymous just as true lovers are light and our universe is the very same. A person not able to maintain this true love will neither be light nor, properly, an inherent part of the universe. Moojie begins to understand the philosophy of the clan and feels alienated from most of his own human associates. For instance when Pappy, his grandfather, tells him that he has been meaning to kill the cat, Anahita, for long, Moojie can tell him, "This is her land, too." (72) For Pappy, Moojie's claim is like Chinese that he fails to understand. The attempt to kill her proves futile as the spirits help it disappear along with the cave in which she lives on. (73) The apparently dead Anahita returns, resurrected (258).

In the Interview, Gregory gives out the inroads she made into the fields of the miraculous and the magical as well as her aversion to following beaten paths in matters of religion, which could be considered socially generated meaning. She also mentions the kind of love that inhabits the world of her novel. In this significant statement one can see how Moojie's portrait took shape in her mind:

> There is a part of me determined to subvert cultural conditioning and mass constructs of meaning. Early on, so much religious, political, social, familial, and material nonsense piles into our young minds. It leads to fear and fear limits our ability to love. Writing *Moojie Littleman* was a way to imagine transcendental love—not romantic or parental love—but the love that leads to miracles and wonders beyond our understanding,

unconditional love that radiates from the very core of our being. I believe humans are wired for this experience and, one way or another, it is our ultimate purpose.

Robin Gregory is careful never to seem to be preaching in the novel. But she is definitely taking the reader eastward, probably making them see through her magical tale that the West needs to pay attention to certain Eastern worldviews and beliefs, some of them similar to the ones we find in Hinduism and Buddhism. It is necessary to grasp more of the spiritual lessons available in the East than merely indulge in consumerist exchange of commercial items. The discourse of her magical realist novel is about how the Oriental, particularly South Asian, way of tackling things can lead to victory and how the typically Western attitude, (as embodied in Henry Littleman, Pappy, and McTavish) ends in defeat. The postmodern world combines the best that is available in the East with that of the West and *Moojie Littleman* is a global and postmodern novel in which the Western reader is being shown the spiritual wisdom of the East. Most magical realism texts, I believe, take the reader eastward, toward the East per se or, alternatively, towards what the East stands for. The postmodernist West is moving towards other parts of the world to give itself what it has been lacking in thus far. Here is how Simon Malpas begins his book, *The Postmodern*:

> Contemporary culture moves at an almost incomprehensible speed. The opportunities and lifestyles open to people in Europe and North America seem to multiply exponentially as new ideas, technologies and fashions appear at ever increasing rates. Space and time shrink almost to nothing as we move around the world at breakneck pace. Civilizations, traditions and forms of social interaction are transformed or even annihilated as borders become more fluid and conventions, customs and ways of life that once distinguished one place from another turn into matters of choice for an internationalised consumer. (1)

The West has currently taken to yoga, meditation and controlled breathing (all associated with India) in a big way. These practices have found acceptance in the occidental peoples' lives, aimed not only at promoting good health but helping in self-realization. Understanding the Self and its connectedness with the universe or "bramhand", man's journey into the cycle of rebirths, and the nature of suffering is an important part of Hinduism and Buddhism. Gregory's novel is largely an attempt to take the reader towards this self-realization. Ninti, the most knowledgeable member of the Light Eaters, has this to say to Moojie, "The same lesson will be waiting for you wherever you go. You can reject what I am saying, of course, and take another thousand *lifetimes* [emphasis mine] to accept it, if you prefer. It is your choice." (260) Ninti has already just told him about awakening his true nature which is similar to self-realization. "You can choose suffering, or you can choose peace. Your greatest purpose is to awaken your true nature, and that nature is merciful. The one you most despise, the one who in your estimation is unforgivable, is your wayshower." (259)

In the universe of Gregory's novel, a communication between the world of the dead and the living is quite possible. When Moojie loses his mother, the parent who has cared for her adopted child, she comes to him and he can feel her spirit distinctly while he is in church: "'She's here,' he whispered." (15) His father can feel nothing of her spirit. And then, "During the closing hymn, the Mamma spirit fell gently over Moojie, a veil of light that warmed him to tears." (16)

Not surprisingly, there is reference to Moojie's mother's ashes. Ashes are normally associated with cremation rather than burial. Hindus and Buddhists, among some others, burn their dead rather than burying them. "Listen," she went on, "do you hear that? 'Tis his mother. She's rolling in her ashes." (17) The novelist seems to be taking the reader to another culture, distant from her own. The little boy, even before entering the age of ten, can begin to see the school of suffering in the Buddhist sense. We know that at the base of Buddhism is a doctrine called the Four Noble Truths. The First Truth is that all life is suffering, pain, and misery. This realization is behind what the stuttering Moojie tells his father: "Don't be sad, Papa. I-If life was all sunshine and chocolate, we wouldn't have any saints a-and we'd never find our way back to heaven." (19)

In Hinduism, bachelorhood (Bramhacharya, the first stage of men's lives) is to be lived in celibacy till the age of twenty-five. Moojie's mother echoes this view when she tells him to keep away from women: "'Girls are like cats,' his mother had once told him. 'When you rush after them they run off. Someday you'll have manly stirrings. You mustn't trust them. Your body will lie to you but your heart will not.'" (62)

Moojie does have the "manly stirrings" for Babylonia but he is told by the Light Eaters that he is to remain with his own people in such matters and he does that. As a result of the several right things Moojie does, he is able to conquer his problems and ultimately cures his paralysis. Besides, as in the Hindu and other Eastern systems, there is talk of pantheons, burning pyres, astrologically conceived stars, and things one would never associate with Western culture. There are Indian and other oriental names and words like "Sanat Kumara", "Lord Babaji", "Uma", "Manish", "Kisha", "Sindabad", and "salam" that one encounters in the novel.

Like other magical realism works of fiction, Gregory's novel takes us through dreams that are revelatory. People, who first appear in dreams, then appear in real life for Moojie. (28-29) Dreams can and do reveal things which the mind fails to grasp and magical realism takes us to these romantic visions. Moojie is first taken to the deep cave where he meets a girl wearing a green veil with an exotic bird perched on her finger. He awakens with icy ears and knows it is a prophecy. "He belonged with the girl and her kind." (28) Later he does find the Light Eaters and Babylonia, the girl he falls in love with. Even in wide wakefulness, the dream feeling persists. "Out here, you can feel the ghosts," Pappy said. "You can feel them hanging in the trees." (29) Mind reading is another form of the magical we encounter in the novel. (190)

Robin Gregory does not look to the East alone for setting up the stage for the drama of her version of magical realism. She seems to be decidedly taking into her basket features of a Western worldview, particularly from fairy tales like *Jack in the Beanstalk* and the poetry of the romantic poet William Wordsworth. It is not only in her mysticism that one is reminded of Wordsworth. She sees the connectedness of the individual to his universe as Wordsworth sometimes did. We are reminded of the poet who spoke of things like, being "laid asleep in body" and becoming "a living soul" and seeing "into the life of things" ("Tintern Abbey"). And his view that "Nature never did betray the heart that loved her" in the same poem, seems to have deep roots in Gregory's mind. Wordsworth's belief in "the unknown modes of being" (*Prelude*), his faith in the child's being "the father of the man" ("My Heart Leaps Up") and his intense fascination for children in weak situations ("The Idiot Boy", "We are Seven", "Lucy Gray", and Wordsworth's cult of childhood which continued well into the Victorian age, can all be found in Robin Gregory's novel. Gregory does talk about her similarities with Wordsworth: "While Wordsworth and I may differ in our names for the consciousness that speaks through nature, we seem to share a consensus that there is a 'voice' or an 'ineffable' presence with whom we can commune." https://robingregory.net/2017/05/26/question-from-a-reader/

There are great similarities between the following lines from the novel and Wordsworth's poems that spiritualize nature:

> He opened the window and sniffed the cool, dry grass, listened to the laughing creek and trilling crickets. He looked and watched... the quivering light, the summer air, the rippling water—the stars, the creek, the moon, it all felt holy to him, there alone in the night with his cat. It was like he wasn't the only one *seeing* something; the universe was, actually, somehow, strangely, mysteriously *seeing* him.... That's love. (46)

These lines have much in common with the thought of the poem, "Tintern Abbey" which is too long to quote in full:

> The sounding cataract
> Haunted me like a passion: the tall rock,
> The mountain, and the deep and gloomy wood,
> Their colours and their forms, were then to me
> An appetite; a feeling and a love,
> That had no need of a remoter charm,
> ...That time is past,
> And all its aching joys are now no more,
> And all its dizzy raptures....
> And I have felt
> A presence that disturbs me with the joy
> Of elevated thoughts; a sense sublime
> Of something far more deeply interfused,
> Whose dwelling is the light of setting suns,
> And the round ocean and the living air,
> And the blue sky, and in the mind of man...

In the mystical vision of Wordsworth, as in Gregory, everything in the universe is connected or fused through nature (Wordsworth's word is "interfused") and the connectedness leads to love.

In Wordsworth's *The Prelude I* (line 420), there is, a significant phrase, "unknown modes of being" that *Moojie Littleman's* magical world echoes. These unknown modes of being are, "no familiar shapes", but "huge and mighty forms that do not live". Wordsworth believed that there were more unseen things around people than the ones they could see. Gregory talks of honoring all life around us, including the "unseen world." (243)

Moojie Littleman is like the typical fairytale character who ultimately manages to achieve his heart's desire by curing himself of his disease and acquiring a position from where he can save everyone else, by virtuous actions. One is reminded of Pinocchio who became a real human being due to his good actions.

II

Just as the American novel, *The Improbable Wonders of Moojie Littleman*, though set in America, goes Eastward in attitude and philosophy, similarly the Indian novel, *The Tailor's Needle*, goes westward by taking the reader into the lives of several Westerners even though the main characters are Indian and they are placed in Indian settings. There are several English men and women that share the stage in this family drama, the saga of Sir Saraswati Chandra Ranbakshi and his family, in a historical setting. The English and Indians are constantly learning from each other in the process of hybridization. In Sir Saraswati is a perfect postmodern character because though he is Indian, with an Indian value-system, he has been educated in England both in school and at the university. A truly global being, he finds it difficult to join the Indian Freedom Strugle initially because of his intense faith in Britain.

The Tailor's Needle seems to combine magical realism with the fairytale; it has several characters with roots in fairytales. The British Viceroy is vain like the Emperor in *The Emperor's New Clothes* and is fooled and humbled by Sir Saraswati's clever plans. The two Ranbakshi sisters, Maneka and Sita, may have their origins in Indian mythology, but they are also like women in fairytales; one active and cruel, the other passive and kind. The dominating Maneka can be cruel and arrogant like Snow White's stepmother; in her worst moments she can become like a spiteful witch. She initially acquires a cruel step motherly role against

Gauri even though she is not her stepmother. Maneka is the sister of Yogendra, the man Gauri loves. Gauri, a Cinderella figure, is from a lower caste, wanting to marry her prince charming, Yogendra, of the highest caste. The marriage seems impossible. After the many ups and downs Maneka suffers, she gets chastened and becomes like the fairy godmother of Gauri, helping her to marry Yogendra. The novel ends with Yogendra and Gauri about to marry to live happily ever after.

The Tailor's Needle is a multi-generic novel that has been compared with the works of Tolstoy, Jane Austen, Boris Pasternak and Agatha Christie by Vinod Joseph (2015). But what is special about this novel is that it contains a different kind of magical realism. The magical realism of this novel is not such an obvious or visible part of it; it is inbuilt into its plot and style. The author does not set out very consciously, or so he claims, to write a work of magical realism, as Gregory does. He probably didn't even know that it would become a novel of magical realism, as he maintains in an interview, and yet magical realism enters this novel through the back door. Maneka, Sir Saraswati's daughter, has insulted and angered a fakir. As if in a fairytale, the fakir's curse changes the life of this daring and difficult woman. After marriage, she is so traumatized in her new home that her effrontery and chutzpah leave her. If such things can happen, then there *is* magic in the air; the kind of magic one encounters in a fairytale or in Shakespeare's *Macbeth* where the plot is affected by what the witches have predicted and in *Othello* where the "magic in the web" of a handkerchief can undo the trust of a husband in an unerring wife. In Part II of *The Tailor's Needle* everything seems to follow as a result of the curse on Maneka. Maneka, who has hooked up a handsome husband with her waggishness and her audacious strategies, and virtually tamed him, before the curse, is reduced to a much weaker second wife after the curse. She is confronted with the presence of his first wife, Meena; a spirit that is virtually a living being. The reader is never made to feel the horror of this. The magical seems to co-exist with the real, the improbable with the mundane. A spirit is presented as the memory of a dead wife, but she is so much a part of the place that she gives the impression of a ghost:

> After Meena life had changed completely at Nadir Palace. Her death had become the only reality of the place; it had become a part of the life that survived there. Maneka had now to coexist with Meena's memories. (167)

The first wife may have been killed by her own husband, but the husband, Mohan, prefers to love the spirit of the first wife rather than his living second wife, Maneka. Maneka must learn to emulate her or lose her husband's goodwill. He does spend a few pleasurable days and nights with Maneka but soon starts behaving oddly, suspecting her growing intimacy with his friend, Dilip, till he is murdered in mysterious circumstances, with Maneka blaming herself for Mohan's murder. It is as though a tigress has turned into a cow. This, when seen in retrospect seems to have happened due to the curse. In this category of magical realism even the plot of the novel is dependent on something as extra-rational as a curse. The curse has taken her to a home where life is tinged with a ghastly experience:

> One of the branches kept rubbing against something and made grating sounds. In these sounds was another sound somewhere in the backyard, the sound of a woman screaming. Maneka got up and tried to see if there was anyone at the window. She heard the tinkling of a woman's silver payals... a woman was walking somewhere close by. This sound would alternate with the sound of the woman screaming. (169)

Thus, though there is an essential similarity between the two novels that makes them hybridized in some sense, with their East-West fusion, there is a basic difference in the kind of magical realism each uses. Gregory's novel has used magical realism more at the level of the content, whereas Sharma's has it more at the the level of form, or structure. For her, the spirituality and the philosophy need to be conveyed to the reader more urgently than reveling in an artistic narrative technique, while for him it is the artistic fusion of genres (historical, postcolonial, multicultural, psychological, the comedy of manners, the gothic, the murder mystery) and an artistic plot.

In an article, "Magic and Realism in *The Tailor's Needle*", Vivek Dwivedi points out that there are few novels that make use of as much magical realism, which is a comment on the manner of narration in which the improbable can be narrated as something mundane. This is an art-related feature. Even the title of *The Tailor's Needle* is metaphorically or artistically conceived:

The "worlding" of this novel is made of some very interesting, though now rather unreal scenes. We are first introduced to a man, Sir Saraswati Chandra Ranbakshi, who is always doing improbable things; who is ready to take on a viceroy of British India and cow him down with his wit, his daring, his political sagacity, and above all his education which has made him into a tailor's needle, a man who is sharp enough to penetrate and stitch together almost every kind of difficult and disrupting situation that he encounters. The tailor's needle is a metaphor that describes a man for all seasons. (731)

Dwivedi compares Gabriel Garcia Marquez and Sharma's manner of narration. Each tells of supernatural worlds as if they were natural and hardly mysterious. (732) The best example of such events in *The Tailor's Needle* is when Sir Saraswati takes his ten-year-old son to Swami Jeevananda's ashram, where the swami narrates things about his present and past lives. The hale and hearty swami tells them that he would leave his body after partaking of some of the "suji halwa" he was cooking. The swami passes away peacefully, leaving father and son stunned. Everything that happens in this scene has different effects on listeners from the East and the West. (42-56) Indians take it in their stride while the English men and women narrativize it over cups of tea. This scene, as Dwivedi points out, is central to the novel's structure and texture as here we come across a swami who can intuit the future of Sir Saraswati and his son. This is the stuff of which magical realism is made.

Interestingly, if *The Tailor's Needle* puts certain improbable, supernatural, happenings into the narrative of the novel as though they were mundane events, to use Salman Rushdie's terms; it does something similar with its non-supernatural events as well. Rushdie had used the phrase, "the commingling of the improbable and the mundane" which has become a significant parameter of magical realism. (Bowers, 3) Making ordinary (not supernatural) extraordinary is what makes this novel unique. Maneka manages to force a British district collector, Larry Stephens, to marry his own maid against his wishes. She then virtually bullies Mohan Kaushik into agreeing to marry her in another wedding. Sir Saraswati forces the timid Seth Tona Mall to prepare for and defeat a dreaded bandit. The novel takes us through unusual happenings as though they were things that could easily happen next door. Sir Saraswati goes on doing these improbable things which are indeed impressive but the narrative makes them look quite probable.

Central to magical realism are intuition, telepathy and such other inner journeys or modes of experience that have helped humankind to perceive what can never be possible when the rational faculties alone are active. *The Tailor's Needle* places the inner over the outer; the intuitive and the visceral over the intellectual. The manner in which Sir Saraswati is able to outwit and defeat the British Viceroy, thrash and conquer the dangerous Jhanda Daaku, solve the murder mystery of his son-in-law reveals a man who has inner conviction, depth and force; and does not rely on his intellect alone.

Sharma is a teacher of literary theories and should have read magical realism well enough. When asked by an interviewer whether Sharma had used magical realism, he tried to evade the issue. He did ultimately say that he did not want to sound like a second-rate Salman Rushdie. He probably saw the kind of impression magical realism has had on Western scholars. Christopher Warnes, for instance, talks about the confusion it has created in his mind; Fredric Jameson and others, like Marisa Bortolussi have given to magical realism a seductive power that cannot be escaped and yet denied it the status of a more realistic fiction. This seems to be the reason why a novelist so deeply entrenched in this mode of fiction does not want to be branded under its label. What follows is from Vivek Dwivedi's "Interview with Lakshmi Raj Sharma" (2011):

> VD: Have you used magical realism in *The Tailor's Needle*?
>
> LRS: I have tried to use no set formula or literary device unless it comes naturally in the narrative. I have used certain features of the British Comedy of Manners, probably… because I had always wanted my narrative to be like fiction rather than seem too realistic.
>
> VD: If you did not want to use realism in *The Tailor's Needle*, then you may have fallen into the trap of magical realism, maybe unknowingly. Do you agree?
>
> LRS: No. Why must you force me to answer this question? I was conscious that I could sound like a derivative Salman Rushdie and therefore I tried to avoid using the device of magical realism in my novel or, at least, his kind of narrative technique.

Sharma then states, in this interview, that India's romantic past is something that has fascinated him no end and he has always marveled at the near-impossible tasks that some Indians of earlier times have performed. *The Tailor's Needle* is actually a collection of such events that have been fictionalized. There were several maharajas in British India, some of whom are portrayed in *The Tailor's Needle*. They seem to emerge out of fairytales. These maharajas were grand people with strange stories attached to their lives. Whatever went on in their palaces was far from what sounds real in our times. The West has in any case often treated Eastern countries as exotic holiday-resorts that provide strange mystical and bizarre experience. This is what Sharma has tried to present through *The Tailor's Needle*, a magical India that few have seen.

One point made by Sharma in another interview (3 July 2013), is interesting. He believes that what is magical for one individual placed in a certain culture may not be magical for another in a different culture:

> On second thoughts, it seems to me that magical realism has entered the world of the novel [*The Tailor's Needle*] surreptitiously. I suppose that magical realism is an alternative way of presenting the reality, reality as perceived by an author of an intuitive bent of mind. The improbable and the mundane co-exist in several parts of *The Tailor's Needle*, with the one entering into the arena of the other. A number of turning points in the novel's plot are based on highly improbable happenings. But what is improbable for some need not be improbable for others. What is magical for the Westerner might be quite natural or real for an Indian. It is probably a question of faith and belief for some—a question that is absent in the case of others.

The Tailor's Needle shows two cultures, the British and the Indian, both of which have been presented with utmost sympathy. This point has been made effectively in a lecture by Sumita Parmar (see YouTube, 5 March 2013) and also shown in a dramatization of a few scenes from the novel, by the teaching staff and students of the Department of English, University of Allahabad. The novel shows a possibility of the the two cultures coming together which most multicultural novels seem to deny. Sharma describes a party in the Mirzapur Club in which there is a French magician showing off his magical tricks to the chiefly British audience. The Westerners are shown enjoying the tricks (not real magic). But the plot goes beyond such clever tricks into a way of life of a certain class of Indians between 1915 and 1950, in which the Indian could reasonably experience a world not governed by rationality and commonsense but by feeling and intuition. The resonance and wonder of a magical world was still alive in India till then. This resonance had the power to evoke enduring images, memories and emotions that seemed real. Here is such a typically resonating passage from *The Tailor's Needle*:

> 'Children, don't be unhappy. You'll be seeing a beautiful river [Ganga] in Mirzapur, a river that can change everything for us.... [It] comes down to us from heaven. Someday I'll tell you about how Bhagirath brought it down to earth for us. The water of this river is sacred and you'll be surprised that it never decays,' said Savitri.
>
> 'Are you unhappy, children?' asked [her husband]. There was no answer. 'Remember, you are a part of a larger system. You are not alone. You may go anywhere but you're still connected to every other place in this world. Nature has blessed us with memories. You can always fly back to Kashinagar on the invisible wings that your minds contain!' he said, a patriarchal tone in his voice....
>
> '...even in a desert of the plains, it is possible to see these green mountains of Kashinagar.' (26-27)

Intriguingly, both the novels see this interconnectedness in the universe. In the magical realism of these two novels there is a more positive attitude than either Modernism or Postmodernism would permit. Instead of accepting the human lot as a lonely, alienated and faithless people, it tends to promote the view that we are well grounded and connected in a rather living universe that is ours and has a moralistic role to play in our lives. Both Gregory and Sharma have painted a rosy picture of *Karma*. Though neither of the novels have the slightest bit of propaganda, each maintains that our actions are responsible for whatever happens.

Fredric Jameson has given us some features of magical realism. He said that it is distinct from realism and, as in Márquez, achieves a synthesis between the surreal and the real. (301) He further considers it to be about peasants and having an "anthropological perspective", coming from left-wing revolutionary ideas, having a Freudian uncanny element and providing a possible "alternative to contemporary post-modernism". (302) This last possibility of providing an alternative to postmodernism, seems the best part of magical realism as a literary genre. But both the novels under discussion, far from providing an alternative to postmodernism, share in some of its features, like having an East-West fusion. *Moojie Littleman* is about peasants no doubt and contains the uncanny element. *The Tailor's Needle* is not a story of peasants but does have the uncanny in it as well. Each of these novels has evolved away from what magical realism has been. In fact, Linda Hutcheon comes up with a more realistic point about magical realism. She believes that magical realism, with its characteristic mixing of the fantastic and the realist "has been singled out by many critics as one of the points of conjunction of postmodernism and postcolonialism." (See Eva Aldea, 8) This conjunction also "hinges on the fact that Hutcheon sees postcolonialism and postmodernism as related by a strong shared concern with the notion of marginalization with the state of what we would call ex-centricity." Ben Okri's *The Famished Road* (1991) is sometimes called magical realist as it combines the world of the spirits with the real world. This novel is both postcolonial and post-modern, in addition, in the sense that Hutcheon has written of magical realism. Hutcheon's conception of magical realism with its marginality can be seen in a novel like Arundhati Roy's *The God of Small Things* which would better fit into this description of magical realism. But both *Moojie Littleman* and *The Tailor's Needle* go beyond the scope of these theoretical conceptions of Jameson and Hutcheon, who wrote on these issues in the 1980s. Some of these opinions spilled over into the 1990s. Ben Okri's novel was published in 1991 and Arundhati Roy's novel came in 1997. Magical realism has clearly evolved beyond that point now, in these recent works, proving Bhabha right. It has brought together the East and the West in both form and content in these two novels.

Works Cited

Aldea, Eva. *Magical Realism and Deleuze: The Indiscernibility of Difference in Postcolonial Literature*. Gloucerter: Continuum Publishing Corporation, 2011.

Bhabha, Homi K. Ed., 'Introduction: Narrating the Nation', *Nation and Narration*, (Oxon: Routledge, 1990), 7.

Bhabha, Homi K. *The Location of Culture*, Oxon: Routledge, 1994.

Bortolussi, Marisa. "Introduction: Why We Need Another Study of Magic Realism", *Canadian Review of Comparative Literature* June 2003, 279-293.

Browers, Maggie Ann. Introduction. *Magic(al) Realism*. Oxon: Routlege, 2004.

Dwivedi, Vivek. "Magic and Realism in *The Tailor's Needle*" *International Journal of Humanities and Cultural Studies (IJHCS)* Vol 3, No 1 (2016) https://www.ijhcs.com/index.php/ijhcs/article/view/1362.

Dwivedi, Vivek. "Interview with Lakshmi Raj Sharma". *Transnational Literature* Vol. 3 no. 2, May 2011, http://fhrc.flinders.edu.au/transnational/home.html 3.

Elie, Paul. "The Secret History of One Hundred Years of Solitude", Jan. 2016, http://www.vanityfair.com/culture/2015/12/gabriel-garcia-marquez-one-hundred-years-of-solitude-history.

Eliot, T. S., "Preface", *Lancelot Andrewes*. London: Faber and Gwyer, 1928, ix.

Faris, Wendy B. "The Question of the Other: Cultural Critiques of Magical Realism", *Janus Head* Vol. 5, no. 2, Feb. 2002, p. 101.

Gregory, Robin. *The Improbable Wonders of Moojie Littleman*, California: Mad Mystical Journey Press, 2015.

Gregory, Robin. "Question from a Reader", 26 May 2017, https://robingregory.net/2017/05/26/question-from-a-reader/.

Jameson, Fredric. "On Magic Realism in Film", *Critical Inquiry* Vol. 12, No. 2 (Winter, 1986), 301-325.

Joseph, Vinod. "Book Review—The Tailor's Needle by Lakshmi Raj Sharma", *Winnowed*, 23 April 2015, http://winnowed.blogspot.in/2015/04/book-review-tailors-needle-by-lakshmi.html.

Malpas, Simon. *The Postmodern*. Oxon: Routledge, 2007, 1.

Obrien, Christian and Barbara. *The Genius of the Few*, Rockville: Borgo Press, 1985.

Pandey, Abhimanyu. "Interview with Robin Gregory". *Writers in Conversation* Vol. 4 No. 7, 2017 https://journals.flinders.edu.au/index.php/wic/article/view/2.

Parmar, Sumita. "Lakshmi Raj Sharma's *The Tailor's Needle* Book Launch" 5 March 2013, https://www.youtube.com/watch?v=OHvXDWaWGO0.

Said, Edward W. *Orientalism*. Gurgaon: Penguin Random House, 2016.

Sharma, Lakshmi Raj. *The Tailor's Needle*, New Delhi: Penguin Books, 2012, Ist. Ed. 2009.

Tiwari, Janmejay. "Postcolonial Writings and Metaphors: *The Tailor's Needle*". *Galaxy: International Multidisciplinary Research Journal* Vol. II Issue IV 3 July 2013, www.galaxyimrj.com Galaxy: International Multidisciplinary Research Journal.

Warnes, Christopher. "The Hermeneutics of Vagueness", *Journal of Postcolonial Writing*, Vol. 41, 1, 2005, 1-13.

CHAPTER TWO
The Question of Voice and Sylvia Plath

The question about the nature of an author's voice seems to have invited more debate than consensual agreement. After Modernist conceptions of voice, more recent theories have branched out in different directions. The tendency in recent times has been to move away from the author to other sources to locate the voice. T. S. Eliot's belief that poetry is an escape from personality could be behind this shift in the perception of the nature of an author's voice. It had been suggested that the voice of an author comes from an author's inner most being. John Middleton Murry, the Modernist critic, spoke of the romantic author's ability to listen to the inner voice, to which T. S. Eliot replied that he himself was inner deaf (Naorem Khagendra). But these remarks arose out of a more than decade long polemical opposition on Romanticism versus Classicism between the two. Khalil Gibran seems to have said something that resembles Murry's view in his poem, "A Poet's Voice Xv": "I stand alone listening to the voice of hope in my deep self…" Though there are far too many views on the nature of voice, this article will restrict its approach to five basic views: (a) James Scott Bell, (b) Les Edgerton, (c) Jane Smiley, (d) Meg Rosoff and (e) Paula Berinstein while trying to discover Sylvia Plath's voice or voices through two of her poems, "Mirror" and "Daddy". Having taken the most acceptable features from each of the five scholars mentioned above, a working formula on the nature of voice will be put together to examine Sylvia Plath's voice(s). This article attempts to synthesize views that describe the nature of voice in as brief a way as possible and then tries to trace Plath's voice to finally see whether this formula works out or not.

Meg Rosoff sees voice as a connection between the subconscious and the conscious minds. For her it is the subconscious mind dictating to the conscious. She is still in the Murry line. Says Rosoff:

Your writing voice is the deepest possible reflection of who you are.… In your voice, your readers should be able to hear the contents of your mind, your heart, your soul.

Jane Smiley, the novelist-critic, believes that language is a great inspiration for a novelist like Dickens (32). For Dickens a character's flow of speech is a flow of self-representation and a flow of wisdom (33). "Characterization becomes the fruit of language rather than vice versa. Dickens's books are peopled with embodied voices who talk first and submit to the plot later" (33). For Smiley, narrative voice is social and is the psychology of relationships. Hence characters directly or indirectly become one of the many voices of an author's narrative voice. The reader who enjoys one or more of the characters is automatically directly connected to one or more voices in the narrative.

James Scott Bell writes that "a voice is symbiotic". The author must identify with the character so closely that he or she feels what the character feels, thinks what the character thinks (17). According to Bell it is assumed that it is the author's voice we are talking about. But according him, in fact VOICE = CHARACTER background and language filtered through the AUTHOR'S heart and rendered with craft on the PAGE (11).

The first two aspects character and author are *symbiotic*. That is, they exist in union and grow together. After that stage of growth comes the final destination on the page rendered through the craft of the page (11).

Les Edgerton believes that the voice of an author is not in plots and characters as it is in the author (5). The author should not emulate someone else or write neutrally as that spoils the telling of the story (10). Further, writing according to rules means losing your voice (13). Following the rules of language (Grammar) can lead to a bland voice (Plath uses little grammar in "Daddy") Your choice of synonym will reveal your style and voice (27). Substituting your word from the thesaurus will get you Mr. Roget's voice instead of yours (25). No such thing as synonym exists (28). Voice is the most important element of style. How you achieve your own voice is governed largely by the words you select to put on the page (26). Raymond Obstfeld compares the authors' voice to Aristotle's definition of "essence"; "the essence of something that special quality without which that something would no longer be what it is" (27).

According to Paula Berinstein a writer's voice is a way of telling a story in a distinctive manner (1). Voice emanates from a persona who tells your story (1). This persona is more than the narrator; it's the unseen hand pulling the strings—the producer who decides what the look, feel and content of the work will be and how it should be perceived by the reader (3). The persona is not the author; it's an artificial personality created by the author on a per project basis (4). An author is always whoever he or she is but an author's personas can be wildly different from each other. In practice, most authors use the same or the similar persona over and over again, but they don't have to. The narrator is not the persona. The narrator executes the persona's directives (6). Voice does not convey the narrator's take on the story, nor the author's, but rather the persona's feelings, beliefs, values and agenda. Why do all these characteristics come from the persona and not the author or the narrator? Because just as an actor isn't the same as the role he or she plays an author isn't the same as his or her personas (8).

It is not easy to put together all the above views on the nature of voice. But certain points can be sifted out from these views to formulate a working formula in order to study the voice of Sylvia Plath on the basis of two of her poems in which there is a persona each who can be said to represent the voice of the poet in part, never entirely, though. The two together come close to what seems to be the poet's own voice.

Voice relates to the inner self of the poet directly or indirectly. Most of the time the voice is not the author's own but is definitely connected with the author. It is the subconscious mind of the author connected with the conscious and hence is related to at least a part of what the author's inner self has perceived. Often a character or a character wearing a mask, a persona, reveals the voice of a literary text. Character and author have a symbiotic relationship. The narrator is not the persona; he is directed by the persona. The text's style can also reflect the voice as the style relates to words and language. Characters and personas are constructed by the language that flows out of them. With this synthesis on the perceptions of the nature of voice, it is possible to look at Plath's poems.

The first poem, "Mirror", is one in which Plath seems under the influence of T. S. Eliot, who believed that poetry should be an escape from personality. It has been suggested that Eliot's theory of Impersonality influenced a number of Confessional Poets of whom Plath was one. This running away from the self is evident also in "Daddy". "Daddy" is a poem which strangely resembles "Mirror", as this poem not only attempts to escape from personality; "Daddy" is a poem which emanates from her personality in part but then proceeds to mislead the reader regarding who the poem is about. In "Daddy", the speaker is a young woman suffering from Electra complex and is rather like though not identical to Plath. (Elaine Connell, 36)

However, in "Mirror" the speaker is the mirror, one who claims to be unbiased and truthful to the point of being exact. It speaks like a male, in love with the wall in front, painted pink, a feminine color. But as the poem proceeds, one learns that the mirror is neither unbiased, nor is it very truthful. It is definitely not exact. The utterances of the mirror construct the picture of a talkative male who is biased against women because he cannot sympathize with an aging woman's problems. The wall remains the same, and relatively unchanged. It is liked because it is incapable of changing like an aging woman who becomes more and more difficult for a man to control or like (in contrast to the more stable wall). The poem is a monologue in which the mirror keeps speaking and also revealing, in the process, that he is no more than what a feminist would consider the typical male to be: one who claims to be just but is not so. During the course of the poem, the mirror contradicts its claim that it has "The eye of a little god, four cornered", because its claim to a godlike objectivity turns out to be a myth.

A point that this article makes is that in "Mirror", there is a message within a message. Even as the mirror says that it is unbiased and objective and has "no preconceptions", the reader can see, in the mirror's reflection, that it is not possible to be unbiased and objective. In the escape from its personality lies the mirror's personality as well as its voice. A deconstructionist would say that there is a contradiction within the poem; the poem undoes its basic premise that the mirror reflects truthfully. In a highly artistic manner, Plath keeps out the words "reflect" and "reflection" from the poem even though that is in a way the subject of the poem. She brings out the double meaning of "reflection" without ever using this word in the poem. This word is absent from the text but as a deconstructive reading would suggest, it is also present in its absence. A mirror may seem to reflect only the truth but in this poem it is doing more than that; it is reflecting like a thinker, or like the poet herself. Yet the mirror thinks like her only partly because it is shown as a male with a critical eye towards Woman. The mirror's narration is what Berinstein considers to be a persona's dictation to it. Yet the mirror's words can also be taken as a character's language that has been dictated by the subconscious mind of the poet, revealing her feelings towards men. Sylvia Plath was one who often thought like a feminist, pointing out what was wrong with men though she could be feminine as well:

> Throughout her poetry Plath demonstrates a vacillation be-
> tween feminine and feminist stances to such an extent that nei-
> ther word can satisfactorily be applied to her writings (Elaine
> Connell 98).

"Daddy" has been considered to be one of Plath's most popular poems (Connell, 34)). The reason for this is not far to seek. It is representative of the poet, perhaps more representative than her others poems. Yet the voice in this poem is not entirely Plath's though it is hers to a large extent. There is also in the poem an "Eliotic" running away from the self. Tracy Brain in her essay about the dangers of reading Sylvia Plath's work as an unfiltered outpour of personal experience has warned us about what we must avoid to misread Plath.

The speaker in this poem is a persona, not the poet, yet there is very little effort on the part of the poet to wear the mask. The speaker comes rather close to Plath's own position and yet tries to escape being exactly like her. The reader who is not very well acquainted with the poet's life but who yet does possess a basic knowledge of it will tend to be misled into believing that the speaker in this poem is a character representing Plath. What Plath has done in this poem is to speak in a voice of a girl who both loves and hates her father. But the father in the poem is not an exact representative of Plath's father, Otto Plath. Though she does say in the poem that the Daddy of the poem stands at the blackboard as Otto Plath actually must have done as he was a teacher:

> You stand at the blackboard, Daddy,
> In the picture I have of you.

But she goes on to emphasize that her father is like a Fascist and possesses every feature of a Nazi as well. A large part of the poem is devoted to comparing Daddy with a Nazi or Fascist, which Otto Plath was definitely not. Hence the target created by Sylvia Plath in the form of her Daddy is an exaggerated version of what her father had been. He may not have had enough time for his family because he was a dedicated and conscientious teacher but that does not mean that he was an extremist as has been presented in the poem. When a poet speaks in her own voice, she normally does not misrepresent whatever she reveals. On the other hand, when a poet wishes to misrepresent someone she creates a persona whose voice becomes the poem's voice. Plath clearly wants to misrepresent her daddy because her attack on him is not a genuine attack; she wants to attack her ex-husband, without doing that directly or very clearly. Here too, like in "Mirror", she tries to deceive the reader by not giving a true picture of what she is setting out to do. Her main purpose is to speak against men, particularly her husband, but she does that by directing her anger against her father instead. A daughter can say virtually anything to a father because that will not lead to the same consequence as would happen if an ex-husband was attacked to the same extent. The persona in the poem therefore speaks as a feminist first and foremost, a woman who will not accept repression either from a father or a husband. By attacking men as represented by the father and the husband, she can say a lot against the husband. Her method is to abuse the father and then say that the husband is like the father. She often targeted men in her poems as she does here in "Lady Lazarus":

> Beware
> Beware
> Out of the ash
> I rise with my red hair
> And I eat men like air.

The Plath-like character through whom the poem "Daddy" is narrated has hidden behind the persona whose voice permeates through the poem. This persona speaks in an exaggerated language, and becomes a more radical version of Plath. What probably happened to her in life because of the circumstance in which she grew up has been stretched out of proportion and the reality is left far behind. The voice in the poem therefore though somewhat like the poet's is in fact is an exaggerated version of her voice and given to us through a persona's rather than in the poet's own voice.

One reason why the hatred towards her father has been expressed more, than the love, is that the poet wishes to make this poem contemporary. The poem is contemporary because of its feministic attitude towards men. Feminism is against patriarchy and it is therefore necessary to unravel a daughter's feelings towards the first male in her life, the father. The persona in this poem seems to mislead the reader by attacking the father to a greater extent than the husband. Maybe if the poem were written entirely in the poet's voice, it would have targeted the husband a little more. Instead she keeps away from bringing this man openly to bash up as she would want to do. She suppresses this desire and gives to us a poem where she talks of killing her father though certain lines give out that she loves him:

> I was ten when they buried you.
> At twenty I tried to die
> And get back back back to you.

She calls her father everything black, including the devil. Her portrayal shows a very genuine hatred for her father. But that is why it is not the poet's own voice, it is a persona's.

Jane Smiley's theory that the voice of a text is visible in the flow of language given to a character in that text, is reflected in the following words of Elaine Connell:

> In Daddy, however, we have the sense of the persona in a triumphant almost exulted state. This is reflected in the language which is no longer the traditional, restrained, poetic diction of the earlier poem but unrestrained, slangy and free:
> "Daddy, daddy, you bastard, I'm through" (Connell, 112).

"Mirror" and "Daddy" together come close to what could be Plath's voice. Each reflects her love for speaking against man and the manmade world. Each targets man indirectly; the first seems to reflect the male attitude by making a mirror say things that men do, against women, while in the second poem the speaker seems to target Daddy when in fact the diatribe is against a husband. Both poems have personas wearing masks who point towards Sylvia Plath's voice but never contain it entirely.

Works Cited

Bell, James Scott. Voice: The Secret Power of Great Writing. California: Compendium Press, 2015.

Brian, Tracy. "Dangerous Concessions: Sylvia Plath". http://www.grin.com/book/126751/sylvia-plath-s-lady-lazarus-cultural-and-social-context.

Connell, Elaine. Sylvia Plath: Killing the Angel in the House. Hebden Bridge: Pennine Pens, 2012.

Edgerton, Les. Finding Your Voice. Ohio: Blue Skies Books, 2012.

Murry, John Middleton. See Ernest G. Griffin, John Middleton Murry. New York: Twayne Publishers, 1969, p. 44.

Rosoff, Meg. The Guardian, Tuesday 18 October 2011. https://www.the-guardian.com/books/2011/oct/18/how-to-write-fiction-meg-rosoff.

Simely, Jane. Thirteen Ways of Looking at the Novel. New York: Random House, 2005.

Singh, Naorem Khagendra. T S Eliot: A Reconsideration, Published by APH, 2001, p. 77.

Simely, Jane. Thirteen Ways of Looking at the Novel. New York: Random House, 2005.

CHAPTER THREE

The Postmodern Hero in
The English Patient and Londonstani

Since the term Postmodernism is riddled with so many contradictions, and since the nature of postmodernist fiction is not without its own share of puzzling assumptions, it is hardly surprising that there is virtually not a single clear account of the postmodernist hero. Linda Hutcheon informs us that postmodernism is the most over- and under-defined term in both current and cultural theory. Attempting to analyze the postmodernist hero cannot be simple because as Hutcheon maintains, "postmodernism is a contradictory phenomenon, one that uses and abuses, installs and then subverts, the very concepts it challenges" (3). And yet postmodernism is a term that has come to stay securely and it cannot be done away with. In a seminar on the Hero and the discourse related with heroes, it would be in the fitness of things to see how postmodernism has affected the conception of the hero.

This article seeks to erect a picture of the postmodernist hero sketching it along with its ambiguities; the picture as it emerges through the sketches of the heroes of two postmodernist novels in mind cannot, however, be considered final or complete. It can be a rough sketch of what the postmodern hero looks like. This article attempts to study the conception and creation of two different versions of the postmodern hero, Almásy (in Michael Ondaatje's *The English Patient*) and Jas (in Gautam Malkani's *Londonstani*), and, in the process, to come to some understanding of how the postmodernist hero is very different from some other conceptions of the Traditional Hero. These two heroes hardly stand out as heroes in the texts they inhabit. The reader has to figure out with great effort and concentration as to how they can be given the status of hero in their respective texts.

To arrive at how sketching the picture of the postmodernist hero is problematized, it is first necessary to see the problems of postmodernism that make it such an abstract term. The term seems to make little sense because it describes the Western world both temporally as well as spatially. In addition, it seems to go beyond the domains of space and time. Brian McHale describes the situation aptly when he says:

> We can discriminate among constructions of postmodernism, none of them any less "true" or less fictional than the others, since *all* of them are finally fictions. Thus there is John Barth's postmodernism, the literature of replenishment; Jean-Francois Lyotard's postmodernism, a general condition of knowledge in the contemporary informational regime; Ihab Hassan's postmodernism, a stage on the road to the spiritual unification of humankind; and so on. There is even Frank Kermode's construction of postmodernism which in effect constructs it right out of existence. (4)

Scholars have tended to see origins of the postmodern hero in Tristram Shandy and Don Quixote. This is another way of saying that the postmodern hero may have a serious burden to carry but his presentation is always lacking in the grandeur of a tragic hero; for him mockery is a primary weapon and he is merely a shadow of a traditional hero, or, even his very antithesis. John Barth is almost always named as a postmodernist novelist, particularly for his fourth novel, *Giles Goat-Boy* (1966), which comically portrays the world as the campus of a university. Barth has written two lengthy theoretical pieces on the postmodern novel. These often-quoted documents are called, "The Literature of Exhaustion" and "The Literature of Replenishment." In the latter, he links postmodernism with a unification of fantasy and seriousness. The *Cosmicomics* (1965) of Italo Calvino are considered truly postmodern by Barth. Barth is to be taken as a key figure in postmodernism because virtually every account on postmodernism names him in postmodernist discourse. Even Ihab Hassan, one of the key theorists on postmodernism, includes Barth in his list with others.

Postmodernists are different to the modernists not only because they succeed them in time but because they are different to and deviate from modernists. Whereas the heroic modernist creates works out of pure imagination, the postmodern artist works with "cultural givens", trying to make the best use of them "in various ways (parody, pastiche, collage, juxtaposition) for various ends. The ultimate aim is to appropriate these materials in such a way as to avoid being utterly dominated by them" (Groden Michael 398). The genres mentioned above are all sometimes present in modernist works too and they have some connection with mockery. The difference between the modernist (Alfred J. Prufrock, for instance) and the postmodern hero is that the former is a medium for mockery whereas the latter like Almásy or Jas is able to be above mockery in the ultimate analysis. Postmodernism which comes from the work of Barth, Salman Rushdie, Alasdair Gray and others continues to concern itself with literary technique playing with "popular cultural reference and pastiche." (Malpas 27-28) Ihab Hassan calls Barth's novel one of the harbingers of postmodernism. What emerges from one of the leading theorists on postmodernism is that it is "fundamentally contradictory, resolutely historical, and inescapably political" (Hutcheon 4). Linda Hutcheon's rather more complete survey of postmodernism in literature (1988) also mentions Barth along with Vonnegut, ECO, Salman Rushdie, as the "exemplars of a postmodern or metafictional literature which deliberately and playfully employs paradox to display its own artificiality and contradictions", which plays with genres and their conventions and alludes to high and popular culture in such a way as to appeal to a very wide audience.

As heroes, Almásy and Jas are both far from heroic. In the beginning of *The English Patient* one gets the impression that Almásy is a soldier wounded in the war, but as the story unfolds it dawns upon the reader that he is actually a desert explorer who has got burned in a plane crash. While Ondaatje tries to keep up Almásy's heroic image by keeping the facts hidden from the reader, we are shown Almásy lying on a bed from the beginning to the end of the novel. Only intermittently are we shown his desert episodes, in flashbacks. His bed is the battlefield for him. In this battlefield of the bed there are moments of romance with Hana the nurse, moments of love alternating with moments of intense suffering that require morphine to calm him down, there are flashes of narration, of diplomacy with the other two men that cluster around his bed. Alongside his manly image there is a time when he seems attracted to the younger, Kirpal Singh. It is Almásy around whom the story revolves and goes on until he finally dies and everything happens in a ruined villa. Interestingly, the ruined villa is in the very geographic location, Tuscany, where the Renaissance began. This according to Barth is one of the features that make a novel postmodern. For Barth, Italo Calvino is like a guiding star for the post-modern novelist. Calvino keeps one foot always in the narrative past—characteristically the Italian narrative part of Boccaccio, Marco Polo or Italian fairy tales and one foot in Parisian structuralist present; one foot in fantasy, one in objective reality. Barth maintains that reading postmodern fiction is like listening to jazz. *The English Patient*, time and again, brings us to the "listening to jazz" feature of postmodern-ism. Here is an example:

> There was no movement from them. She broke free of the chords and released her fingers into intricacy, tumbling into what she had held back, the jazz detail that split open upon notes and angles from the chestnut of melody.

> *When I take my sugar to tea*
> *All the boys are jealous of me,*
> *So I never take her where the gang goes*
> *When I take my sugar to tea.* (Ondaatje 68)

Jean-François Lyotard stresses the fact of how the postmodern world is a globalized situation in which "Anything Goes". Rather than nationalism there is an internationalism that seems to be the order of the day. The hero of *The English Patient*, Almásy, is the best example of this phenomenon. His nationality is kept hidden for half the novel. He appears to be English but turns out to be Hungarian. Of-course there is nothing even quite Hungarian about him. He seems to be a citizen of the English-speaking world. The world of this hero is a relaxed mul-ticultural world where literally anything or any person can fit in. The others who interact with him are from Canada and India and each is as much at home in this Italian villa as the other. Nationalism, which may have been such a vital consideration in the World War that is drawing to a close in the background of the novel, has suddenly become a non-issue. The hero of *Londonstani*, Jas, even more, is shown as one lacking in a national identity. Just as we have considered Almásy to be English for half the length of the novel, we consider Jas to be Indian until the very last chapter when we get to know that he is actually an English-man who does not want to be identified as an Englishman. His parents are pained at the prospect of their son wanting to disown his British identity, but he continues to want that. The postmodern hero can be seen as one without a national identity; he is a citizen of the world, if there is such a person. History has shown shifts down the ages. The modernist was a nationalist, but not so a number of postmodernists.

Hayden White and, following him, Linda Hutcheon, have shown how in the nineteenth century history and literature were two branches of the same tree. However, now the situation is different. This separation of literature and history has been subjected to postmodernist debates that challenge the separation. Postmodernist theory and art foreground what the two domains of literature and history share rather than what they do not:

> They have both been seen to derive their force more from verisimilitude than from any objective truth; they are both identified as linguistic constructs, highly conventionalized in their narrative forms, and not at all transparent either in terms of language or structure; and they appear to be equally intertextual, deploying the texts of their past within their own textuality. (Hutcheon 105)

The English Patient is a postmodern novel according to all the features mentioned in the lines quoted from Hutcheon and most specifically because of the intertextuality it contains both from history (Herodotus) and literature (Stendhal, Kipling, James Fenimore Cooper who authored *The Last of the Mohicans,* and others). The hero of *The English Patient* seems neither historical nor entirely literary. He is indeed a clever mixture; a combination of both.

John A McClure points out that Almásy's position is dramatically postmodernist in its "celebration of the nomadic, loosely collective and uncentered styles of being" (176). For McClure, both Hana and her beloved patient, Almásy, produce "new testaments". Hers is a kind of "postwar existentialism" and his is a kind of imagined war fought on his deathbed. It is important to recognize, Malpas informs us, that postmodernity is itself already a discourse that is fractured and fragmentary (5). It follows from this that in an age fraught with a fractured and fragmentary discourse, the postmodern hero cannot be heroic or complete. Almásy is shown as a patient, who is no longer the powerful explorer he once was, his is a fractured existence, one that will lead only to death, but the memories of his past, shown in flashbacks, constantly contradict his fragmentary existence. Jas too has a weak existence throughout the novel till he is beaten up and he becomes a hospitalized patient. He is weak in contrast to Hardjit and Ravi, and then even much weaker than Sanjay. Yet it is his story, his desire for a South Asian girl, and his loss that the novel has focused on. We seem to celebrate his weakness, his loss and the discovery of his true identity. Postmodernism is said to question distinctions between high and low culture through the use of pastiche, the combination of subjects and genres not previously deemed fit for literature. *Londonstani* aptly does this by presenting the uncultured rudeboys as though they were fit to be considered heroic.

Postmodern literature, as is well known, relies heavily on narrative techniques such as fragmentation, irony, paradox, and the unreliable narrator; and often is defined as a style or a trend which emerged in the post-World War II era. This makes it similar to modernism. But whereas modernism seems to crack down under the fragmentation, postmodernism accepts fragmentation as a cultural given; a situation that virtually celebrates it. Both novels under focus, *The English Patient* and *Londonstani*, are monuments of the unreliable narrator; they are obscure because of their fragmentation and revel in irony and paradox. In *Londonstani* Jas, the narrator of this novel is both the teller as well as the tale of *Londonstani*. This makes the narrative rather distinctive and complex. Instead of focusing on the inner workings of the characters' minds, Jas focuses on the external details which offer the reader a realistic perspective of the characters leaving moral judgment to the readers. He himself is continuously judged by the reader.

An important factor about the narrator of *Londonstani*, Jason, who is confusingly called Jas, until the last chapter when we discover that he is a Brit and not an Indian, is that he is a weak man; pitiably weak and a helpless person. Such a weak person can become a great narrator in a novel. His lack of strength and personality makes him self-conscious enough to withdraw and become inward looking. Such a person may seem to be a part of the main action that is carried out by the seemingly extrovert others, but he is in fact observing everyone minutely because they seem smarter and stronger than him. Malkani, in a smart move, creates a unique narrative where he makes an Englishman seem like an Indian (the novel has this ironic structure) and tells us everything from the point of view that is neither Indian nor English. This turns out to be a great narrative skill for a multicultural novel. Jas is a "coconut". This term had been earlier used by E. M. Forster in a short story for a gay Indian character. It is used for Jas to reveal his inner whiteness as opposed to his external crudeness and hard look, a kind of hybrid personality who can sympathize with both races.

The postmodern hero should be seen in the light of what Jean Baudrillard and others have termed as hyperreality—a failure of the consciousness to make a distinction between reality and a simulation of reality particularly in technologically advanced societies. It is seen as a condition that stitches together the real and the fictional. Almásy and Jas are both highly realistic creations but in both there is something that makes them no more than the simulation of reality. All the heroics of Almásy become so different once his identity of a desert explorer is revealed. Similarly, Jas, who has posed to be an Indian so realistically has been merely simulating something that he is not.

Like in Barth's *Giles Goat-Boy*, the humor in *Londonstani* and many events of the book are frequently in extreme poor taste, employing a number of potentially offensive representations of South Asians and women. The language of the novel particularly is poor to the extent of being off-putting even though in this kind of language lies the novel's soul and literary content. That the English patient, László de Almásy, is a patient is no coincidence. He is presented mostly as a patient in a form that is far from heroic. He does possess some heroic qualities though these are shown in flashbacks not as his present reality. Similarly, Jas in Londonstani, is the very opposite of the hero of a classic written before the postmodern existence of human beings registered itself in some minds. The typical postmodern hero is constructed linguistically through broken forms of narrative and dialogue that can match his actual being. Almásy and Jas are thus created through uses of language that are far from regular and their settings are created through a fusion of literariness and historicity.

Lyotard's *The Postmodern Condition* (1979) is largely about the knowledge of how contemporary societies work. States are beginning to lose their power and multinational firms are beginning to get more important than the erstwhile powerful governments. In *Londonstani* we see this tendency of the Indian rudeboys to virtually worship the multinational companies and products, and reveal a lust for various kinds of cars. Jas is always with the Indian rudeboys narrating their stories in trying to earn quick money to rise in a world where the erstwhile powerful Britain can be ignored and even condemned in favour of a multinational consumerism.

The postmodern hero can be seen as a distant cousin of the antihero and the Byronic hero no doubt, but he is also constructed on the cross-sections of fiction and history. The study of Historiographic Metafiction makes it possible to understand the true nature of the postmodern hero. Therefore, this article makes use of some of the theoretical frameworks provided by postmodern minds such as Hayden White, Jean-François Lyotard, Jean Baudrillard, and Linda Hutcheon.

Works Cited

Barth, John. "The Literature of Replenishment—Postmodernist Fiction" Nov. 19, 1998. http://english.fju.edu.tw/lctd/asp/works/304/study.htm.

Groden, Michael, Martin Kreiswirth and Imre Szeman. *Contemporary Literary and Cultural Theory*. Baltimore: Johns Hopkins Press, 2012.

Hutcheon, Linda. *A Poetics of Postmodernism: History, Theory, Fiction*. New York: Routledge, 1988.

Malkani, Gautam. *Londonstani*. London: Fourth Estate, 2006.

Malpas, Simon. *Jean-François Lyotard*. Oxon: Routledge, 2015.

———. *The Postmodern*. Oxon: Routledge, 2007.

McClure, John A. *Partial Faiths: Postsecular Fiction in the Age of Pynchon and Morrison*. Georgia: University of Georgia Press, 2007.

McHale, Brian. *Postmodernist Fiction*. London: Routledge, 1989.

Ondaatje, Michael. *The English Patient*. London: Bloomsbury, 2004.

CHAPTER FOUR

Showcasing Masculinity: The Kite Runner

One of Hosseini's great perceptions given in *The Kite Runner* and in *A Thousand Splendid Suns* relates to the imbalance between the roles of males and females in the Afghan society. Men and women complete human life together and the absence of one gender's contribution can lead to a devilish kind of existence as is happening in this country. Women are shown as no more than child producing and male-supporting instruments in Afghanistan. They are absent from the decision-making or administrative setup of the nation. Hence the society as it emerges is the very opposite of what the multicultural vision of society has been, at least on paper. Theoretically, multiculturalism strives for respect of every individual, for human rights, where men and women are to be given some kind of equality. Afghanistan is therefore shown in the novel as a kind of antonym to the multicultural society in America.

The Kite Runner demonstrates how not all Afghans are able to assimilate multiculturalism and blend into the American society in an appropriate manner. The one who goes through an education, a different kind of socialization, in America, and acquires the necessary flexibility of a multicultural being is the one who can survive and live gracefully in America. What has sometimes been missed out by critics of this novel is the fact that Hosseini sees multiculturalism as a tendency that seems to incorporate what may be called a reduction in the masculine traits of human beings. Afghanistan, as it is portrayed in this novel, possesses a hideous kind of maleness that is almost synonymous with savagery. This quality must be reduced in anyone who wants to live amicably and harmoniously in America. Because Amir is not very manly to begin with, he fits in with the multicultural setup rather well in America and it is then that he becomes more respectable in his eyes. This helps him to gain the confidence to return to the ruined Afghanistan and help his nephew, Sohrab to escape from the clutches of the Taliban male society. In this novel it seems that extreme masculinity is the binary opposite of the multicultural. For this reason, it is necessary to study the three males Hosseini has sketched adroitly in this novel. To put it crudely, multicultural socialization is seen as a kind of taming process; something that takes away the negative aspects of excessive masculinity. This kind of masculinity is to be found in Baba and, to an extent, in General Taheri, both of whom never blend in fully with the life-style required in a multicultural set up. Amir's flexible nature, and less masculine personality, helps him to succeed much better in the multicultural setup in America. Hosseini equates the obnoxiously masculine world of Afghanistan with a virtual savagery. The novel seems to oppose rigidity, orthodoxy and fundamentalist extremism, each of which is unfortunately a part of the hard-boiled nationalist denizen. *The Kite Runner* is postmodern in its support of an international rather than a national attitude and order. This novel can be considered a commentary on the vices of nationalism.

A nation like Afghanistan is built on brutally male forces, where only the most powerful and physically able will survive. There are very few women in this nation, a fact that makes this world more savage. The multicultural world of America is less male because women have more power here and are less exploited by a male infested society. The novel does show nationalism in a negative light.

Hosseini has an eye for how the human lot can be divided even within a nation. The Pashtuns speak of the Hazaras as though they belonged to another species. Even historical discourse presents them as such:

> The book said part of the reason Pashtuns had oppressed the Hazaras was that Pashtuns were Sunni Muslims, while Hazaras were Shi'a. The book said a lot of things I didn't know, things my teachers hadn't mentioned.... It also said things I *did* know, like that people called Hazaras *mice-eating, flat nosed, load-carrying donkeys.* (8)

It is a male world in Afghanistan where everything is right or wrong according to what the Afghani *male* believes in. In Afghanistan, "Real men didn't read poetry—and God forbid they should ever write it!" (17) The masculinities projected through the novel are significant as they lead to a kind of gender discourse on how these masculinities of Afghanistan do not blend well with the multicultural world of America. It should be remembered that "masculinities are not equivalent to men; they concern the position of men in a gender order. They can be defined as the patterns of practice by which people (both men and women, though predominantly men) engage that position." (Connell) The entire novel is tinged with a multicultural hue because the narrator of the novel, Amir, is an author living in America after spending his childhood in Afghanistan, like Hosseini did. He has seen both cultures and has acquired a unique multicultural vision in his narration. We are always looking at the novel's universe through this double vision of one who has seen and known both cultures from the inside. Amir shows us Afghanistan like a guide shows people tourist sites. The novel is in substantial parts what is called literary tourism. But this literary tourism shows an awareness of what the Westerner would like to see in Afghanistan or in the typical Afghani male. This is one of the reasons for this novel's huge success in the West. It sold 38 million copies of *The Kite Runner* and *A Thousand Splendid Suns* together by 2007.

Baba has brought up the boys, Amir and Hassan, on a policy of "broaden your minds and attitudes." This would lead to Amir's ability to accept America wholeheartedly as is required in a multicultural setup. Baba's and Amir's attitude is pretty secular as is required for multicultural co-existence. Baba, we are told, mocks the story behind Eid, just like he mocks everything religious (67). Amir's responses, particularly his doubt about the existence of God, is pretty postmodern. "If there was a God, He'd guide the winds, let them blow for me so that, with a tug of my string, I'd cut loose my pain, my longing" (57). Living in Afghanistan, Baba comes up with a number of anti-Islamic suggestions and practices. He takes them to several Western films so that they are familiar with a number of significant Hollywood male heroes like John Wayne, Charles Bronson, Steve McQueen, Clint Eastwood and others. But Amir's reading in his childhood has been rather unwestern. He has been brought up on a hybrid view of the world, a fact that helps him to evolve further into western values when fate takes him to America.

Khaled Hosseini has given the world a novel with a highly complex structure. It doesn't only tell a story in a masterly manner but also presents us multiculturalism from different perspectives. It spells out what kind of individual will fit into multiculturalism without fear or favour and what kind will not. Hosseini has shown the degree of civilization and acculturation that is necessary for multicultural life to function smoothly and successfully. He has put into the plot of the novel the process by which a society or nation reaches an advanced stage of social development and organization. As something of a marvel in narrative art, consciously or otherwise, Hosseini has created three male characters that symbolize three states of human evolution and development. These three demonstrate that none of the three states can be considered perfect. The reason why this chapter gives so much space to the three main male characters of the novel is that multiculturalism has been shown in this thesis to have a direct bearing on gender. Hosseini's novel is an eye-opening document to the fact that too much maleness will be inimical to the success of a multicultural setup. This is what is rotten about the nation of Afghanistan; it has suppressed the feminine side of life and therefore accepted extremist philosophies with open arms. The three main male characters, Baba, Hassan and Amir, need special attention as they have been conceived with a multicultural vision. Hassan may never have gone to America, but he is the one male with that perfect balance between male physical courage and its opposite ability to be accommodating. This perfect blend is most required in a multicultural setup. The novel reveals who the perfect male for the multicultural society is, but it also shows us how multiculturalism takes away the freedom of individuals. It curbs nationalist sentiments and it suppresses individual growth in a sense; a growth which if allowed to proceed negatively, can go in terrorist or extremist directions.

Multiculturalism may be what the postmodern situation demands to make people inhabitants of a global village but it certainly cannot be described as the ideal or perfect kind of human arrangement because it comes at a price. It tends to mentally enslave a free people to support what the West has stood for. It also shows that though people, who migrate in large numbers to countries like America, manage to keep up their national and cultural peculiarities even in the foreign land to an extent; they never blend entirely with the country they have migrated to. In an interview (RFE/RL correspondent Courtney Brooks) Hosseini points out how different Afghani migrants to America learn and adjust differently:

I think it was an even more difficult adjustment for my parents to be uprooted and to have lost everything they had worked their lives for, and to have to restart their lives essentially from scratch and to try to restart a life in an environment that was dramatically different from the one they were accustomed to.

That said, I think they also had a very healthy sense of perspective in that we were among the extremely fortunate Afghans who were allowed to restart our lives in America, whereas millions of Afghans ended up living in refugee camps in Pakistan, lived as laborers in Iran or elsewhere in the world. So we were quite, quite fortunate.

The chapter also brings into light certain useful points made by scholars such as Mousumi Paul, Jessica Keally Luckhardt and Tarana Parveen in examining the scope and nature of multiculturalism as inlaid into the pages of *The Kite Runner*. From Paul's work it can be seen that the apparent simplicity of Hosseini's text is deceptive inasmuch as he self-consciously brings about an "inter-text" of multicultural studies. Jessica Keally Luckhardt introduces us to the concept of "cultural competence" as used by Hosseini, Linda Hogan and Arundhati Roy in their novels. Cultural competence, we are told, is a skill for navigating and examining societies such as the diverse American society. These novels are particularly well-suited to build cultural competence because of the deep and emotional connection that readers find to the texts. These novels are constructed in ways which lead to heightened reader responses, "utilizing the perspective of youth, time devices, and storytelling to engage the reader in an interactive and transformative reading experience." Together with thoughtful instruction, relating to multiculturalism, they hold the capacity "to transcend their literary value and contribute to cultural awareness and social change." Parveen makes it clear that even as Hosseini knits multiculturalism into his novel, he actually introduces us to the cultural problems of Afghanistan.

Sarah Kinne has some interesting points to make about Amir's handling of his changed situation in America after having been brought up in Afghanistan: "How does Amir navigate the various socioeconomic and racial spaces of Afghanistan and the United States by utilizing multiple subjectivities?" She compares Hosseini's novel with Gloria Anzaldúa's mixed-genre work *Borderlands/La Frontera*. Her discussion of Amir's subjectivities at once brings her work in line with the views of Bhabha on the question of subjectivities just stated. This aspect will be discussed later in this chapter.

The Kite Runner is a painful account of a nation in the grips of terror, evacuation and migration. The novel also showcases multiculturalism in a radically new perspective. This chapter analyses Khaled Hosseini's narrative art in portraying the pain of leaving one's country and settling in another. It also examines this unique perspective, or point of view, on multiculturalism that Hosseini acquires in the novel. It shows how Hosseini keeps a limited eye on the issue of diaspora and is able to maintain the focus on a nationalistic discourse even as he narrates the tragic tale of an Afghan family that needs to escape from Afghanistan at a historic moment of political change and cope with a multicultural setup in America. Hosseini's novel reveals a divided nation in the clutches of social hatred where the ethnic Pashtuns consider it their birthright to exploit and rule over the Hazaras. The Hazaras are the have-nots that are ever subjugated and oppressed. This society has an inner multiculturalism as the Pashtuns, though living in Afghanistan, are united with the Pashtuns of Pakistan, rather than the Hazaras of their own country. Pakistan is home to the largest section of the Pashtun community. Hazaras make good servants to the Pashtuns and their women good bedmates to them, if the story of the novel has truth.

The picture of Afghanistan, after its political change because of the Russian and Talib intrusions, is tragic indeed. Till all had been well, kites flew and scored the skies of Kabul. This is a symbol of the wellbeing of the nation. But then the scene changes and kite-flying becomes a thing of the past. The landscapes have changed with rubble visible all around and almost no trees remaining in a place where trees abounded. Everything changes under the new political arrangement. Freedom for the individual is also a thing of the past. People can be seen hanging from beams in the roof of restaurants (226). The best example of the change that has set into Afghanistan can be seen in the the fact that an erstwhile university professor, who was a colleague of Amir's mother, has now become a beggar:

> The old beggar nodded and smiled. Revealed a handful of remaining teeth, all crooked and yellow.... 'I used to teach it [a Hafez ghazal] at the university.'
> 'You did?' (218)

Assef describes the condition of Afghanistan as he accuses

Amir for deserting it, "Afghanistan is like a beautiful mansion littered with garbage, and someone has to take out the garbage" (249).

The old man coughed. 'From 1958 to 1996. I taught Hafez, Khayyam, Rumi, Beydel, Jami, Saadi. Once I was a guest lecturer at Tehran, 1971 that was. I gave a lecture on the mystic Beydel. I remember how they all stood and clapped. Ha!' (218)

The novel is unique in that it shows how people in Afghanistan are so nationality-conscious. Here is a passage that shows this aspect: "The Russian soldier said something to Karim, a smile creasing his lips. 'Agha sahib,' Karim said, 'these *Roussi* are not like us. They understand nothing about respect, honor'" (101). Then again Amir tells us how Baba has been affected by leaving his country and settling in America: "It was living in America that gave him an ulcer" (109). Baba distrusts the Vietnamese couple, just as they do him (111). "Fuck the Russia!" Baba shouts as he sits and has beer with people of other nations, mainly Americans. (115)

Hosseini has given a graphic description of how Afghans often live in America as second-rate citizens. They hardly contribute to the life of America in any substantial way, unless, of course, they have received their degrees in America. They do only the most uninviting things possible in their multicultural existence:

> On Saturdays, Baba woke me up at dawn. As he dressed, I scanned the classifieds in the local papers and circled and circled the garage sale ads.... Baba drove the bus, sipping hot tea from the thermos, and I navigated. We stopped at garage sales and bought knickknacks that people no longer wanted. We haggled over old sewing machines, one eyed Barbie dolls, wooden tennis rackets, guitars with missing strings, and old Electrolux vacuum cleaners. By midafternoon we'd fill the VW bus with used goods. Then early Sunday mornings, we drove to the San Jose flea market off Berryessa, rented a spot, and sold the junk for a small profit. (119-20)

The result of this dull existence in America leads to a lot of nostalgia for the homeland. Amir's father-in-law, the general, makes an interesting observation: "Well people need stories to divert them at difficult times like this" (121). The general then begins to think and tell about the time when Baba and he hunted pheasant together one summer day in Jalalabad when it was discovered that Baba's eye was as keen in the hunt as it was in the business (121-22). The novel contains several passages of nostalgia for Afghanistan. When Amir returns to Afghanistan, he sees its corrupted and destroyed state; when he is in America he thinks of the happy days in Afghanistan that are no more.

In *The Kite Runner*, we are almost never shown the posh side of America, except perhaps, the advancement in the medical sciences, to an extent. One gets the impression that Hosseini, though disturbed by the corruption and violence that has set into Afghanistan, is still interested in painting a not very bright picture of America; we are shown the imperfections of America. As a result, Baba who had loved the idea of America, never loved America as he might have. Amir tells us in one of his conclusive statements about Baba, "Sometimes I think the only thing he loved as much as his late wife was Afghanistan, his late country" (136).

The narrator in *The Kite Runner*, Amir, begins by telling us about Afghanistan and how his family reacts to it, in the initial stages of the novel. He then migrates to America, gets educated and Americanized, and then talks about the changed and destroyed Afghanistan from there. The change in the point of view from which the story is narrated makes all the difference in the narration. It also gives us a different insight into the nature of multiculturalism. This is one of the highpoints in the novel's art.

Once in America, there is a change of mind at times. The most horrible aspects of Afghanistan are remembered with a sense of nostalgia even as their dreadful reality is never forgotten. We are never made to forget that if things are not right in Afghanistan, they are not right because of the Russians or the Talibans. It is as though the Talibans were not Afghans. They are seen as outsiders that have disturbed the peace of Afghanistan. The saddest thing about Afghanistan is that when the Northern Alliance took over Kabul between 1992 and 1996, different factions claimed different parts of Kabul:

> "If you went from the Shar-e-Nau section to Kerteh-Parwan to buy a carpet, you risked getting shot by a sniper or getting blown up by a rocket—if you got past all the checkpoints,

that was. You practically needed a visa to go from one neigh-
borhood to the other. So people just stayed put, prayed the
next rocket wouldn't hit their home." He told me how people
knocked holes in the walls of their homes so they could bypass
the dangerous streets and would move down the block from
hole to hole. In other parts, people moved about in under-
ground tunnels. (174)

The narrative art of *The Kite Runner* lies in large part in the fact
that people are first and foremost humans, before they are Afghanis,
Pakistanis; Pashtuns or Hazaras. How the Russian invasion can make
them work against their own brethren is a point taken up in the novel.
How blood is thicker than the ties of a social class, and in the family of
the protagonists how a Pashtun will go against Pashtun in support of
a Hazara where there are emotional and familial ties. The basic pattern
perceptible in the novel is that multiculturalism is a system invented
by man for the sake of convenience; it shows people coming together
socially only for convenience. In fact it is a marriage of convenience
where differently cultured people unite expediently and break up when
the relations begin to sour. The novel is, in its ultimate analysis, a book
that foregrounds Afghanistan; a nation mutilated beyond recognition
by power-hungry insiders and outsiders. However, when Hosseini
paints this dismal picture of Afghanistan, he actually invites us to see
how human nature works. We may condemn a certain people, living
in a certain stage of history, but ultimately all people are the same,
because human nature is largely the same everywhere and has to be
reformed by civilizing forces.

Homi K. Bhabha's words in *The Location of Culture* seem to echo in
this novel's background:

These "in-between" spaces provide the terrain for elaborating
strategies of selfhood—singular or communal—that initiate
new signs of identity, and innovative sites of collaboration, and
contestation, in the act of defining the idea of society itself. (2)

The above lines from Bhabha aptly sum up "those moments or processes that are produced in the articulation of cultural differences" in
which Hosseini creates and builds up the characters of Baba and Amir.
The father and son have managed to transport themselves to the soil of

America, landed in the terrain of cultural difference, fitting their lives into the in-between spaces that Bhabha refers to. Baba, who was no real nationalist at home in Afghanistan, has carried his nation with him, as it were, to Fremont city in California's San Francisco Bay Area. He has loved more the "*idea* of America" than America itself, which has given him a carcinogenic ulcer (109). One reason for Baba's leaving Afghanistan is that he has lived with the guilt of producing an illegitimate child and now that child has left him to suffer alone. Baba tries to suffer life in America without Hassan in front of his eyes rather stoically. But he has to pay the price; he becomes a patient and dies.

The Kite Runner is the story of three men, mainly; it is a novel about "masculinities"; how Afghanistan is a male nation where woman's voice is little heard. The lives of each of these three men help in completing the picture of the male society in Afghanistan and then how this purely male attitude is incompatible with the multicultural setup in America. It would be wrong to believe that the novel is no more than these three aspects of its nationalism, transnationalism and multiculturalism. No novel is all thought and idea, and *The Kite Runner* is a number of other things as well: (a) Hosseini's primary reason for its composition is to tell the story of a family of three men: Baba, Amir and Hassan who are each connected in different ways to the nation of Afghanistan or to American multiculturalism. (b) Then, it is the heartbreakingly sad picture of a nation being destroyed due to its own inner cultural decay and due to foreign intrusion. (c) It is about blood being thicker than water and how fathers are related to sons, legitimate or not, and the lies they tell about their relationships. These familial relationships are also indirectly or directly connected with the nation and are controlled by it. (d) It is about guilt and about human nature generally; it is also about redemption and the extent one might go to get the redemption. (e) Surprisingly, it is also about authorship and about reading; how these emanate from a person's character and are related to it. In short, it is a highly complex novel that includes three main strands of thought: nation, manhood and human nature are tied together in society.

A nation and nationalism are not what they appear to be in the present moment. But it is made of a past time; a history and a culture, as well as myths and stories that far predate the present. The immediate plot-structure of *The Kite Runner* stems out of what has happened in Baba's life, before the novel actually begins, his aristocratic background and the masculinities that Afghanistan has prided in. Benedict Anderson, as quoted by Bhabha in *Nation and Narration* has this to say of Nationalism:

> What I am proposing is that Nationalism has to be understood, by aligning it not with self-consciously held political ideologies, but with large cultural systems that preceded it, out of which—as well as against which—it came into being. (1)

A nation and its males and their masculinities are closely related, particularly where there are deep chasms between its social classes. Hosseini has tended to portray how the male has done everything for the self and little for the other sex in his other novels as well. Any narrative worth its salt will tend to maintain that men are behind most of what happens in and to nations. A woman's interference in the nation's political happenings is possible only in enlightened democracies or primogeniture monarchies. David Glover has this to say about nations and masculinity:

> Masculinity… requires careful definition, a discriminating eye. It may be rooted in social class, but class is a matter of birth and breeding, of what one is, not of what one achieves: its highest good in the nation, yet some nations including his own… are prone to "excessive national feeling", falling into vulgar and demeaning posturing, and failing to give the enemy his due. (88)

Much of the novel's art lies in the way Hosseini pits nation against transnationality and multiculturalism. To do this, he creates three characters of a family: Baba, Amir and Hassan. There may be few or no novels in which individuals are symbols of aspects of a nation. Through the character portrayals of these three we get to know about how firmly rooted and closely related nationality, masculinity and familial bonds are. But we go beyond family bonds, to arenas where pressures such as those of society, nationalism and multiculturalism dig into the very base of the family. We are reminded that family is a social institution and has a very different meaning outside a society. Society requires legitimacy and class-line sympathies and even the most well off and socially important personalities will need to surrender to these social needs. Society, masculinity and family are further linked firmly with the nation particularly in societies where patriarchal considerations reign supreme. Baba's is the character that Hosseini has constructed with utmost care to present his fictional thesis of what could be called (a) the institution of the family, (b) the social stratifications of Afghanistan during the nineteen-seventies, (c) the fragile male-dominated nationality of Afghanistan at the point in history covered in the novel, and (d) the clash between American multiculturalism and Afghan masculine nationality.

Baba is an aristocrat of the Wazir Akbar Khan district of Kabul and he is pretty conscious of his social status. His wife, Sofia Akrami, whom he loved, has died in the child birth of Baba's legitimate son, Amir. Baba has therefore found it difficult to forgive Amir for being responsible for his wife's death till they are in Afghanistan and till fate has not forced them to migrate to America. Like a typical male of a masculine society, Baba has slept with the wife of his Hazara servant, Ali, the result of which is his illegitimate son, Hassan. Ali has brought up Hassan like his own son after his wife, Sanaubar, has left him and Baba has kept Hassan's parentage a closely guarded secret. He cannot ever acknowledge Hassan as his own son, but does love him a little more than he does Amir. Hassan's fate keeps him ignorant of the identity of his father. He believes that he is a Hazara whose only duty and responsibility is to be true to his Pashtun master as well as the master's son, Amir. Neither Amir nor Hassan is aware that a common father has sired them; they do know however, that the same woman, mother of neither, a Hazara, midwife, has breast fed them both.

Baba has always been a self-willed man. He has been a grand old man (not old in terms of age but as a person) for whom his self-pride and his own principles have mattered. He has never bowed down to social pressures unless that meant the loss of his social prestige. He has always shown outstanding courage. He has physical courage in abundance. He has once wrestled with a bear (11). His nickname is, "*Toophan agha*, or 'Mr. Hurricane.'" Fear is absent from his dictionary. He has hated the mullahs, saying that he could urinate on their beards. "Piss on the beards of those self-righteous monkeys" (15). Unlike other orthodox Muslims, he drinks scotch whiskey and German beer. He eats pork, something that very few Muslims would do (16). He has manly tastes like playing soccer; he even flew to Tehran to watch the World Cup on television as there were no TVs in Afghanistan in 1970. But he does have his share of social responsibility; he contributes very generously to an orphanage after having it constructed (17). Of course, it is difficult to tell whether he does this because of his guilt in having produced Hassan outside a legitimate wedlock and left him little better than an orphan. On his own, however, he tries to secretly help Hassan as much as he can emotionally and with presents without letting the cat out of the bag about his illegitimacy. Perhaps he would have donated to the orphanage even if Hassan were not his son. Baba is rather individualistic and doesn't need to learn from society. In Afghanistan he is out of sympathy with the social setup of his country; in America he tends to behave like an Afghani who refuses to bend down to the demands of a multicultural setup. In a sense, he is out of place in both countries and his person reflects the fact that multiculturalism does not succeed with every individual.

Baba's fault has been that he wants his son, Amir, to behave exactly as he wants him to. He wants him to be athletic and if Amir is not that, he should at least have interest in games and be a spectator if not a player. Amir's interest in writing or in reading books is not something a typical Afghan male would appreciate; definitely not Baba. His friend Rahim Khan tries to point out to Baba that he ought not to force his children in a particular direction: "Rahim Khan laughed. 'Children aren't coloring books. You don't get to fill them with your favorite colors'" (19). Rahim Khan even calls him "self-centered" (19); he was the only one who could dare to do that to Baba on his face.

Baba, who has lived like a lord in Afghanistan, cannot adjust as he ought to in America. America has not welcomed this kind of individual with open arms either. What he and his son could do in the new country was "selling junk for petty cash... menial jobs" and "grimy apartments—the American version of a hut" (264). Baba keeps reacting to people in America, quite overlooking the social codes of a multicultural existence. He refuses to be treated by a doctor merely because he is a Russian and almost roughs him up for no reason but that he is a Russian settled in America.

Baba's sons, Amir and Hassan, do have something of his nobility in them though each is radically different to him as well. Hassan is illegitimate but thankfully does not know it. He is in a unique position; he has received so much love from Baba that he has begun to consider Baba's family his own. He has been made to believe that he is not equal to Amir as he is a Hazara boy who can never become socially equal to a Pashtun, which Amir is. But Hassan has the blood of a Pashtun flowing in his veins and that makes him a highly self-respecting individual even from childhood. Never having received maternal help or womanly emotions, he is growing up as a male who will never bend to ask for anyone's help. In this he is like Baba. He knows his position in Baba's household and never asks for more than is meted out to him.

With Amir, Hassan has a very special relationship. He is at once both friend and servant to him. What neither of them knows is that they are half-brothers. Hassan cannot imagine a situation in which Amir can succumb to any kind of harm or discomfort. He feels that it is his responsibility and his alone, to save Amir from any misdemeanor or wrongdoing. More importantly, Hassan is Amir's kite runner. There is no one who can beat Hassan at this game. He can get a kite cut loose in a tournament from virtually anywhere because he has learned the art of studying where a kite is going to land. The child Hassan is like Amir's lieutenant, always with him but always second in command. They are of the same age and therefore they have a perfect chemistry with each other in normal circumstances.

Hassan is intellectually even more alert than Amir. He may not have had the same schooling but there is a native intelligence in him about which Amir is more than conscious. Hassan is not only a great listener to the stories Amir writes but is also a fine critic; he can find fault with whatever is illogical or wanting in Amir's stories. He is also a keen listener to the stories and poems of well-known authors that the Afghans consider classical and legendary. He is totally engrossed in these literary works and is always after Amir to read them out to him. He could predict that Amir's literary merit would be recognized by the world someday: "Some day, Inshallah, you will be a great writer... and people all over the world will read your stories" (160). His ability to perceive this literary merit seems to be much ahead of the social class, of Hazaras; it came from his genetic lineage with Baba, the lineage that led to Amir's becoming an author.

To be an Afghan meant to understand the social class to which he belonged. Hassan never knew that he was Baba's son and hence believed himself to be a Hazara even though he had Pashtun blood in him. He did have the courage of the higher class; he was more courageous than Amir. Hosseini has tried to make a myth of the belief that the suppressed are less brave. Hassan could protect Amir and himself when confronted by the three anti-social boys led by the villainous, Assef. He helped Amir throughout his life in some way or other and showed the kind of courage that would be considered exemplary in Afghanistan. Hassan stands out physically and morally in a nation where everything is decaying.

In Hassan's character is contained the story of the Afghan nation, in a slightly more subdued form than it is contained in Baba's character. The chief problem in Afghanistan, as it appears in the novel, is that it is a layered society with the uppermost layer consisting of a class that exploits. It is either a foreign nation, Russia, or a native group of the Taliban, that has taken over the role of the exploiter. The next in the social order is the class called the Pashtuns; the more well-to-do lot in the country, considered superior culturally. After them in the social hierarchy are the Hazaras. The Hazaras are the have-nots in every sense, victims of depravity. Baba has lived in this kind of setup and learned how to adjust with the moral corruption that goes on. He is human, with his own share of faults, but on the whole a man who is courageous and seems to be above pettiness and wickedness. Hassan has imbibed a number of Baba's features and some of those of Ali, the Hazara, whom he presumes to be his father. He has the heart of a generous noble, the dutifulness of the humblest of servants, the loving loyalty that comes from blood relationships, and the grandeur of spirit seen in a few chosen leaders. Hassan has never erred, it would seem, and it would be difficult to find someone like him in real life; he is too good to be true. It cannot be said of Hassan, however, that he is too unreal a creation. People like Hassan are there in rare situations, particularly in backward societies, where powerlessness and poverty have kept them humble instead of driving them towards criminality. His genes are no less responsible for the kind of person he has turned out to be. His is a genetic blend of a Hazara woman, Sanaubar, and a grand Pashtun man, Baba. He has inherited the humility of the Hazaras and the self-pride of the Pashtuns. But he is more than that because Baba is more than what the typical Pashtun is and Sanaubar turns out in the end a caring repentant woman. Hassan has inherited much from his parents no doubt but he has evolved and become one of the few Afghans who are concerned about the plight of their country. He has tried learning how to read and write and become a literary reader. He has used his literacy to educate his son, Sohrab. He is conscious of what Afghanistan is turning out to be and from the letter he writes to Amir it is not difficult to see that he is a nationalist of a high order:

Alas the Afghanistan of our youth is long dead. Kindness is

gone from the land and you cannot escape the killings. Always
the killings. In Kabul, fear is everywhere, in the streets, in the
stadium, in the markets, it is part of our lives here, Amir agha.
The savages who rule our *watan* don't care about human de-
cency. The other day, I accompanied Farzana jan to the bazaar
to buy some potatoes and *naan*. She asked the vendor how
much the potatoes cost, but he did not hear her, I think he had
a deaf ear. So she asked louder and suddenly a young Talib [the
Talibans had taken over power in Afghanistan] ran over and hit
her on the thighs with his wooden stick. He struck her so hard
she fell down. He was screaming at her and cursing and saying
the Ministry of Vice and Virtue does not allow women to speak
loudly. She had a large purple bruise on her legs for days but
what could I do except stand and watch my wife get beaten? If
I fought that dog he would have surely put a bullet in me and
gladly! Then what would happen to my Sohrab? The streets are
full enough already of hungry orphans and every day I thank
Allah that I am alive, not because I fear death, but because my
wife has a husband and my son is not an orphan. (189-90)

The above words not only reflect the chaotic state of absolutist
leaders in Afghanistan; they reveal the sensitive mind of one who has
learned to suffer quietly in a nation where individualism is dead and
the ordinary citizen is without any rights.

Hassan has learned to suffer quietly even from early childhood
when in a shameful incident he is physically assaulted by Assef and his
two other Pashtun friends when the three have overpowered him by
defeating him with physical strength or greater numbers. Amir has quietly watched this incident from a distance and this has made him guilty
for life. In a nation of brute male-force he has stood apart and been a
powerless spectator. Hassan has suffered for being born a Hazara; he
is ignorant of his paternal Pashtun blood which oozes out of his dress
after the satanic boys have raped him. In the end, Hassan turns out
to be a symbol of the exploited, and what is rotten, in the corrupted
nation of Afghanistan. He is a picture of sacrifice from beginning to
end. His life is dedicated to to cause of his Amir *agha* and finally goes
in trying to protect Amir's house, which has been sold to Baba's friend,
Rahim Khan, but which nonetheless, is still Amir's in Hassan's mind
and needs his care. He may be seen almost as a Christ-figure. He does

not complain when Amir falsely accuses him for stealing his watch. In fact he allows Baba to believe that he has stolen it so that Amir may not be proved a liar and false accuser. He does not want Baba to punish him at all for doing so much for spoiling his image. Hassan also never lets anyone know that he had seen Amir hiding and watching him being raped. He and his wife, Farzana, are brutally killed after he has shifted to the house Baba had constructed in the Wazir Akbar Khan district, and which was "thought the prettiest house in all Kabul" (4). Hassan may never have been to America or another multicultural nation, but he seems to have the spirit of multiculturalism deeply and naturally built into his character. With all the physical and moral courage that he possesses, he has that added and rare merit which makes him flexible enough and gives to him the ability to serve society. He has in him inherently what multiculturalism tries to induce into people externally through education and socialization. He has sufficient respect for women as is seen in his relationship with his wife, Farzana. More than that, he can accept and support a mother who had deserted him in his childhood without seriously questioning her behaviour and action. Hosseini could have created Hassan to show what an ideal attitude towards one's opposite gender should be. In both his early novels he has shown a more than critical eye for the male who disrespects the other gender.

The third male in the narrative of *The Kite Runner* is Amir, the narrator of the novel. If Baba represents the aristocratic class of Afghanistan and Hassan its exploited class, then Amir's stay and education in America has made him the true embodiment of American multiculturalism. Hosseini has portrayed nationalism, transnationalism and multiculturalism in a very idiosyncratic manner. He has represented nationalism and its upkeep by relating it to a male dominated setup; he has shown how transnationalism can lead to a great deal of cruelty if it is in the hands of an unenlightened lot; and how multiculturalism can be no more than the arrangement of fear generated by transnational movements and settlements. Multiculturalism is shown as the arrangement to counter fear. Amir has grown up to become an embodiment of fear and guilt. For him multiculturalism is the best fit, the most appropriate arrangement. We get the feeling in this novel that multiculturalism is synonymous with people of more than one nationality co-existing within a social arrangement where people have been able to overcome the inconvenience and fear of cohabitation. But multiculturalism doesn't quite work out perfectly for someone like Baba who has lived like a lord in Afghanistan. People like him are unable to live as restrained and disciplined citizens living transnationally under the banner of a multicultural society. It turns out to be an arrangement in which someone like Amir fits in beautifully but one like Baba does not. Multicultural subjects live in a condition that is between assimilation and transnationalism in a way that challenges our ability to theorize them, and the multicultural nation-state's capacity to recognize and engage them. This theoretical idea is found in Ashley Carruthers's article.

Amir has grown up in the middle of certain fears. His mother died in delivering him and his father has always considered him responsible for his mother's death. As a result, his father has never treated him with the respect he has deserved. Baba is not an ideal father in Amir's childhood. He has shown a slight preference for his other son, Hassan, a fact that Amir finds difficult to understand. Amir believes that Baba is not very happy with him first because of his mother and then because he is not the kind of boy who will develop into a manly citizen that the nation of Afghanistan requires. He has decided to make a great sacrifice to get into the good books of Baba and he does that by finding a justification for not helping Hassan in his time of trouble. His fear has been the main reason but he tries to convince himself that he was trying to make a mark on Baba's mind:

> I ran because I was a coward. I was afraid of Assef and what he would do to me. I was afraid of getting hurt. That's what I told myself as I turned my back to the alley, to Hassan. That's what I made myself believe. I actually *aspired* to cowardice, because the alternative, the real reason I was running, was that Assef was right. Nothing is free in this world. Maybe Hassan was the price I had to pay, the lamb I had to slay, to win Baba. Was it a fair price? The answer floated to my conscious mind before I could thwart it: He was just a Hazara wasn't he? (68)

Hassan better seems to fulfill that requirement. Baba, however, does begin to like Amir a little more after he wins the kite-flying tournament; this makes him appear a better fit for a male dominated world. After migrating to America, Baba begins to bend more towards Amir as he is the only person who sympathizes with Baba entirely, loves him and cares for him in a country where Baba is learning to adjust.

The Multicultural setup of America allows much more freedom to individuals than the orthodox male society of Afghanistan does. Hence Amir can grow up more naturally, in spite of feeling that he has been a coward in Afghanistan. In fact in this alien land he develops the kind of courage and confidence that Hassan had developed naturally in the home country. This is the power of multiculturalism when it functions positively. It makes Amir what he could never have become in Afghanistan. It is difficult to visualize how the Amir of his guilty and fearful childhood could become the daring hero to set free and bring away Sohrab from his bondage in Afghanistan. There seems to be no real cause for this transformation in Amir except that he has been able to get rid of his fear and guilt due to the positive role of education provided to him by America. Thus Hosseini reveals the positive role of multiculturalism; multiculturalism saves Amir and the lack of it kills Baba. Multiculturalism seems to be hardly less than a religion for Hosseini.

Amir, as an American multicultural citizen, has understood perfectly how to co-exist with people different to him. Therefore, when he has to return to Afghanistan to get Hassan's son, Sohrab, out of the clutches of the Talib, Assef, he makes the necessary adjustments easily with virtually all the people he encounters: "As an Afghan, I knew it was better to be miserable than rude" (201). He knows what is needed in the brutal nation that Afghanistan has turned into and he bends himself accordingly. The Afghan nation has become one which makes its people consider themselves outsiders in their own country. But Amir, who has begun to consider himself a tourist in his own country, can still think of it as his own to some extent, to Farid's surprise, because he has acquired the flexibility that multiculturalism imparts to people:

> "I feel like a tourist in my own country," I said, taking in a goatherd leading a half-dozen emaciated goats along the side of the road. Farid snickered. Tossed his cigarette. "You still think of this place as your own country?" (203)

Amir has acquired a hybridity that multicultural existence has imparted to him. Because of this he can feel at home in both countries; definitely in his own alienized country. Bhabha discusses this phenomenon with reference to Parsis but it equally applicable to Amir:

Parsis have always been travelling and translating, then, using the language of colonialism for trade. They therefore have a hybrid identity, something marked by an uncanny ability to be at home anywhere, an ability that always might become the burden of having no home whatsoever. The uncanny, Bhabha suggests, is also the *unhomely....* It is then connected to cosmo-politanism—specifically what Bhabha calls *vernacular* cosmo-politanism, which opens "ways of living at home abroad and or abroad at home." (Huddart 79)

Works Cited

Bhabha, Homi K. *The Location of Culture*. Routledge, 1994.

———. *Nation and Narration*. Routledge, 1994.

Brooks, Courtney. "'Kite Runner' Author On His Childhood, His Writing, And The Plight Of Afghan Refugees: Interview with Khaled Hosseini." 21 June 2012 https://www.rferl.org/a/interview-kite-runner-afghan-emigre-writer-khaled-hosseini/24621078.html.

Carruthers, Ashley. "National Multiculturalism, Transnational Identities." *Journal of Intercultural Studies*, vol. 34, issue. 2, May 2013, pp. 214-28.

Connell, Raewyn. http://www.raewynconnell.net/p/masculinities_20.html.

Glover, David, and Cora Kaplan. *Genders*. Routledge, 2000.

Hosseini, Khaled. *The Kite Runner*. Bloomsbury, 2011.

Huddart, David. *Homi K. Bhabha*. Routledge, 2006.

Kinne, Sarah. "Negotiating the Self: Multicultural Identity in Anzaldua and Hosseini". http://www.academia.edu/8844451/Negotiating_the_Self_Multicultural_Identity_in_Anzaldua_and_Hosseini.

Luckhardt, Jessica Keally. "Building Cultural Competence Through Multicultural Fiction". http://thescholarship.ecu.edu/bitstream/handle/10342/2832/Luckhardt_ecu_0600M_10140.pdf.

Parveen, Tarana. "*The Kite Runner:* Role of Multicultural Fiction in Fostering Cultural Competence". https://www.rjelal.com/3.2.15/160-166%20Dr.%20TARANA%20PARVEEN.pdf.

Paul, Mousumi. http://www.boloji.com/index.cfm?md=Content&sd=Articles&ArticleID=14697.

CHAPTER FIVE

Narrative Skills, Language and Dialogue in Gautam Malkani's Londonstani

It is necessary to first establish that this novel is a work of literary fiction and not a badly written document that freely uses expletives in both Hindi and English. It therefore needs more textual analysis. The novel has a unique voice and uses an inimitable kind of language, narrative, and dialogue. It is indeed an exclusive kind of literary text that carries a distinctive form of multicultural fiction. It goes on to show how gendered roles, particularly the roles of women, come under a cloud in multicultural setups. This has been shown by Gautam Malkani in *Londonstani*. The women characters are given little space and are dimly sketched in comparison with the men.

In *Londonstani*, London is uniquely chosen as a space for multiculturalism as Malkani tells James Graham in an interview:

> I think London is important insofar as it provides the characters with a metropolitan identity. I was really interested in the way that metropolitan identities can transcend other identities in the same way that your national identity can supplant your ethnic identity, or your racial identity or your religious identity.

A question that may come to the reader's mind is why is *Londonstani* included in this book even though its language is hardly right to be a part of a syllabus for the study of literary fiction? The reason for the inclusion of Gautam Malkani's novel in this volume is that it projects a unique category of multiculturalism that no other novel does. This novel will appeal to few readers not only because of its weird, distasteful, language but also because it hardly has a plot that would keep a reader glued to its pages. Instead, the reader is likely to find it difficult to appreciate its narrative and the dialogue that are a substantial part of the narrative. Its publisher, had expected it to be a bestseller, but it turned out, in the view of James Graham, to be a commercial failure of sorts:

> By mid-June 2006, a month and a half after its launch, the novel was among the top 30 bestsellers having sold 4,350 copies. Though clearly disappointing given the publisher's high expectations, these figures are far from negligible given the unpredictability of the literary hardback market. Furthermore, contrary to McCrum's belief that the novel had already been airbrushed from history in May 2006, *Londonstani* has, with some success, been redirected toward the very niche that he believed it had overshot. Malkani is still being invited to give readings and talks at festivals, schools and universities two years after the hardback publication and nearly a year on from its paperback release.

And probably it has not sold more than 20,000 copies till now. It was expected to be a commercial success but wasn't one. However, it has achieved a rare kind of success. It has caged in its pages what no other novel has in an equal measure; it has captured the life and culture of those South Asians, particularly Indians, whose parents migrated to London to earn the fast buck there and produced a breed of youngsters who do everything to make themselves a nuisance by the language they use, the delinquent acts they get involved in, and the threat they pose to the general suburban life in and around Hounslow. However, even in the world of these "rudeboys" who use unparliamentarily language, there are some principles, certain hybrid social norms that govern them. In the words of the *Londonstani: Reader's Guide*, rudeboys include certain "teenage boys of South Asian descent who live in a world of flash cars, name-brand clothes, and self-conscious attitude."

In a language that is utterly new, Gautam Malkani takes us to the roots of a human world, where the outer society plays as little a role as possible. We see young men in an elemental state, speaking without thinking sufficiently and acting without deliberating enough. It is a world that combines a particular kind of people whose multicultural bearings make them rather savage in word and deed. It is a condition in which the bane of this hybridization comes to the fore. The novel puts together the worst of the Indian population alongside the cultured others, trying to prove that even they have an existence that needs to be noticed.

This chapter studies not only the unique kind of multiculturalism that emerges from this novel; it also studies Mulkani's use of language, which is vulgar and irritating no doubt, but it is a marvel of literary achievement at the same time. It carries the experience and feelings of a section of young Indians whose parents settled in Hounslow, West London, in the latter part of the second half of the twentieth century.

Language is a functional entity. It keeps accommodating whatever comes its way. From catering to the needs of SMS messages to the creation of rhetorical expression, it stretches itself out to suit every need in its vast stretch of varied applications. There is a little that language seems to reserve for literary fiction as well. It should not be thought that the term "literary fiction" has a particular fixed meaning. Far from that, the language of literary fiction is once again a vast territory. But we may say comfortably that one criterion that remains pretty constant in the nature of literary language is that it creatively evolves to serve a certain purpose.

Some scholars have gone to the extent of supporting bad and vulgar writing in fiction. They could be marginally justified in what they say because fiction is different to other literary genres in that it can lack in precision and in the other requirements of poetry. Amongst these there are two significant names, pointed out by David Lodge; Marvin Mudrick and Ian Watt (28). According to Mudrick, "In prose fiction the unit is not, as in poetry, the word, but the event.... great fiction can survive, not only translation, but a measurable amount of bad or dull writing in the original" (As quoted in Lodge 28). Ian Watt points out another feature of the language of fiction. He says that a novel's language is more referential than in the rest of the forms of literature. This means that it is meant to refer to other things and is not that important for its own sake. Watt suggests that novelists from Richardson and Balzac to Hardy and Dostoevsky have often written "gracelessly, and sometimes with downright vulgarity" (as quoted in Lodge 28). Lodge points out, in addition, that novels are lengthy documents, particularly the ones written by the authors pointed out by Watt. As in epics, their length becomes a hurdle in the way of a faultless use of language.

But this is where Gautam Malkani's *Londonstani* becomes an important point of reference for our purpose. Its language does not fall in the category of the novelists pointed out by Ian Watt; it is not "grace-lessly" written. One might say that it is disgracefully written for a read-er whose mind and ears are attuned to reading chaste, restrained and decorous English. But the language of *Londonstani* achieves something precisely by the use of this kind of ugly English. It takes the reader to a particular place—Hounslow—a particular place, a borough of West London, where a number of second-generation youngster-settlers from India have been somehow growing up, being schooled and learning to become less than proper and honest citizens. In chapter 27, the word "showdown' is used frequently to show how the life of the "rudeboys" is actually nothing but a showdown that they are trying to express through a certain kind of protest. Far from being like normal people, their ac-tions and speech make them out to be case studies in psychology. They suffer from something like what Lacan considered the mental illness of psychosis and this causes them to act in a certain undignified way. Multicultural co-existence in London is part of the reason for their psychosis-like condition. The language of these rudeboys can seem vul-gar and unpalatable to a number of readers. However, this language can also be seen as a marvel, of what F. R. Leavis referred to as an "explor-atory creative use of language." F. R. Leavis has not only referred to the genre of the novel as a "dramatic poem", he has more importantly stated that the moral responsibility of literature is to be "on the side of life" (Lodge 69). Gautam Malkani is absolutely on the side of life when he gives to these youngsters the language that so realistically and con-vincingly portrays their morbid existence. These youngsters from India and thereabouts have settled in England, become a part of the hybrid culture which is neither here nor there, and create a most negative im-age of themselves. They are a tragic lot in the end. Malkani narrates virtually everything through dialogue. There is a narrator, Jas, who has joined the group of criminals referred to as "rudeboys" and is the most central character in the novel. It is his plight that the novel foregrounds more than anyone else's.

Malkani is at least superficially against the South Asians because in spite of their realistic portrayal, that does make them appear tragic at times, they seem rather wrong in whatever they do. He has cleverly made the Brit member, Jas, first look like an Indian. When our sym-pathies are with him, more than his other Indian friends, he turns out to be English. Without doubt, Malkani's portrayal of the South Asians makes them a petty lot and his selection of this group of Indians shows that though he has studied their lives closely, because he was a resident of Hounslow, he does not have anything really good to say about them. Whereas London was considered to be the cultural capital of the world, Malkani shows these youngsters as people living in the least sophisticated part of London and adding a great deal to make it less sophisticated.

Every novelist worth his salt tries to create a time and place related picture frame different to every other novelist. It is in and through this time/place picture frame that he best tells his unique story. It is this that makes him known and it is this that reflects his individual and idiosyncratic personality. *Londonstani* is the outcome of a need; the need to tell the world of how a certain space, in Hounslow, set in the twenty-first century, is different to the rest of the world, at a particular time in the history of Indo-Brit relations and settlements. In this narrative style and linguistic choice is reflected a certain kind of politics; peoples' desires and distastes, successes and failures, hatreds and attractions. Malkani's need as novelist relates to communities of people trying to share a time and a space multiculturally, and how this sharing is upsetting the applecart of some that are nationally or generationally different. Malkani is at pains to provide newness to the form of the literary expression he has chosen to adopt. He does this by manipulating two basic parts of the novel's structure: (a) the language and (b) the manner of narration. Today's novels, particularly those written by ambitious writers looking for awards of the highest kind, that will fetch them instant fame, have an eye on the invention of a narrative technique and vocabulary that has an imprint of their personalities on them. It is not only new ideas put into new language; it is a race against others to be different and to excel in their difference. It is this effort which makes Salman Rushdie, Arundhati Roy, Julian Barnes and others stand out and seem more successful than others. Julian Barnes is one of the few novelists who describe what the novelist feels as he writes along; he is perhaps describing this feeling of a fiction writer trying to capture the sense of the time as it is shown in fiction or as he has chosen to uncover it in his novel, *The Sense of an Ending* when he writes:

> We live in time—it holds us and moulds us—but I've never felt I understood it very well. And I'm not referring to theories about how it bends and doubles back, or may exist elsewhere in parallel versions. No, I mean ordinary, everyday time, which

clocks and watches assure us passes regularly: tick-tock, click-clock. Is there anything more plausible than a second hand? And yet it takes only the smallest pleasure or pain to teach us time's malleability. Some emotions speed it up, others slow it down; occasionally it seems to go missing—until the eventual point when it does go missing, never to return. (3)

Gautam Malkani has made this kind of effort to capture a time and a place with its difference to all other times and places. Whether he has done this successfully or not is difficult to determine. But it has to be admitted that the language which seems offensive and vulgar at the beginning of the novel affects the reader in a way that he begins to accept and even probably enjoy by the time that the novel ends. By this time, the reader has begun to recognize and even own the ugly reality of the youngsters living in this part of West London. Such is the force of literary fiction.

It is necessary to appreciate as Paul Cobley points out that even the most "simple of stories is embedded in a network of relations that are sometimes astounding in their complexity" (2). This should not be taken to mean that "those relations are beyond the ken of all but the most technically oriented academic minds. The opposite… is the case" (2). Cobley makes a valid point when he says that the "most familiar, most primitive, most ancient and seemingly most straightforward of stories reveal depths that we might hitherto have failed to anticipate. That we do not anticipate them… because we do not attend to the network of relations in which a story resides…" (2) but this does not mean that we do not reach these depths and the potential pleasure they yield.

Gautam Malkani has hit upon a great formula to keep his literary novel going. Even though there is a very bare plot, the novel goes on merely on a narrative that is built out of a dialogue and language that is colloquial. He has found a form and content that go hand in hand perfectly. The form incorporates a realistic description of the setting with the help of a realistic dialogue packed into the narrative; the content showcases the multicultural issues that are part of the Indian and other South Asian youngsters' lives; those youngsters who have to live in London because their parents chose to settle in the district of Hounslow. It is rather evident that most of these rudeboys suffer from something close to "psychosis" in Psychoanalysis. Psychosis is defined in clinical psychiatry as a serious mental illness affecting the whole of the personality. This is different to neurosis; psychotics often do not have an awareness of the morbidity of their condition. They cannot be brought round for treatment consensually and may therefore need psychiatry. Some people with psychosis may also experience loss of motivation and social withdrawal. One of the symptoms of psychosis that is particularly the case with some of the rude boys is disorganized speech.

Interestingly, Jas, the narrator of this novel is both the teller as well as the tale of *Londonstani*. This makes the narrative rather distinctive. Instead of focusing on the inner workings of the character's minds, Jas focuses on the external details which offer the reader a realistic perspective of the characters leaving moral judgment to the readers. He himself is continuously judged by the reader.

An important factor about the narrator of this novel, Jason, who is confusingly called Jas, until the last chapter when we discover that he is a Brit and not an Indian, is that he is a weak man; pitiably weak and helpless person. Such a weak person can become a great narrator in a novel. His lack of strength and personality makes him self-conscious enough to withdraw and become inward looking. Such a person may seem to be a part of the main action that is carried out by the seemingly extrovert others, but he is in fact observing everyone minutely because they seem smarter and stronger than him. Malkani, in a smart move, creates a unique narrative where he makes an Englishman seem like an Indian and tell us everything from the point of view that is neither Indian nor English. This turns out to be a great narrative skill for a multicultural novel. Jas is a "coconut". This term had been earlier used by E. M. Forster in a short story for a gay Indian character. It is used for Jas to reveal his inner whiteness as opposed to his external crude and hard look, a kind of hybrid personality who can sympathize with both races. Malkani achieves his total effect by a three pronged strategy: (I) The narrator is a weak and hybrid looking character; (II) the language used in the narration has several features that distinguish it from the language of other literary texts; (III) and the vastly dialogic nature of the narrative leads to more immediacy and "showing" rather than "saying". "Dialogic" refers to two aspects of this novel. The first is that it is largely in dialogue form and secondly there inheres in it what Mikhail Bakhtin makes out of the term, "that words *in use* have to be understood as always engaged in 'dialogue' with other words: words in practice, whether written, spoken or only thought are necessarily embedded into the social context"(Morris 164). Each of the above mentioned three aspects of the narrative will be examined below.

I. A Well-Chosen Narrator in *Londonstani*

Gautam Malkani's entire novel has a single narrator; a character in the novel, we call Jas, believing him to be a "desi" Indian till in the very end we discover that he is English, not Indian, bearing the name, Jason Bartholomew-Cliveden. This narrator is the antihero in a novel that lacks an actual hero. Jas, though a first-person narrator is somewhat different to other first person narrators, say to a narrator like Jane, in *Jane Eyre*, because the Indian identity with which he begins changes in the end of the novel when we realize that he is English. Then, he often uses "we" instead of "I" in some parts of the novel, making him a first-person plural point of view narrator. His age is nineteen and he is a "white, male" (340-341). The language used to describe Jas, like everything else is not proper English but a hybrid English used by some youngsters of Hounslow called "rudeboys" in the novel. Jas describes himself as a problem: "Problem number three: motherfuckin me" (26). He is suffering from psychosis in the Lacanian sense, as some of the other rudeboys are. He acts as a "batty" a slang for a "mad" person. But this insanity is not the insanity that drives someone to an asylum. It is that quality, which keeps someone from being a worldly, smart and successful person; one who depends on other smarter people. Jas tells the reader:

> I was a skinny wimp [a weak cowardly person], I was embar-
> rassin [embarrassing] to have around if ladies came by, I wore
> crap clothes, I used to have braces on both my upper and lower
> teeth, I'd read too many books, I walked like a fool, I had this
> annoyin [annoying] habit a sniffin [of sniffing] all the time, I
> couldn't usually talk proply [properly] and even when I did I
> couldn't ever say the right thing. Basically I was just generally a
> khota [donkey] like that coconut... (26)

Jas is often protected by the tough "rudeboy", Hardjit. Hardjit takes care of Jas just like a Bollywood hero, ShahRukh Khan for instance, has to take care of the underdog in front of all the ladies (27). However, it may not be right to consider Jas as someone only weak. He has derived his strength from his other two tougher friends, Hardjit and Ravi. He has become a spirited being, even in his narration, because of the constant support he gets from his two friends. Left to himself, he is different. Whatever the mental and physical state of Jas, he is brought before us like the nineteenth century novel narrator, as a realist. This realism in a narrator can work wonders according to Paul Cobley:

> In the nineteenth century, realism and the novel developed into the major narrative form that is often the focus of attention… The realist novel has commanded attention because it has been so supremely concerned with social setting (Snow 1978), because it allowed the the development of a 'great tradition which was 'alive' to its time (Leavis 1962), because it embodied the aspirations of the emergent and then dominant bourgeois class (Lukács 1969), because it rationalized consciousness of time and space (Ermarth 1998) and because it provided domestic pleasures (Showalter 1978). (88)

Realism is the ground that has bred some great fiction just as its opposite modes of narration have also done particularly in the twentieth and twenty-first centuries. Malkani has given to the reader a highly realistic picture of the lives lived by South Asian youngsters who have made West London their home, and if Lacan is right, seem to have become patients of psychosis. Realism can portray the ugly as well as the pleasant realities of people's lives. Literary realism, in contrast to idealism, endeavours to represent familiar things as they are. Realist authors depict routine banal activities and experiences, instead of using a romanticized or similarly stylized presentation. Malkani's realism makes no effort to romanticize the lot of the South Asian rudeboys dwelling in Hounslow. Instead, he projects the ugliest realitiesof their lives,along with those that they seem to enjoy, through a narrative mode which is very original. In the originality of this realistic mode of narration lies the literary content of the novel. However, after Lacan's theories of the real, the imaginary and the symbolic, it becomes necessary to be conscious of the limits to which the real can ever be achieved. David Macey's commentary on Lacan's theory of the "real" could be helpful:

> The real is not simply synonymous with external reality, and

nor is it simply the antonym of "imaginary". It exists outside or beyond the symbolic, is menacingly homogeneous, and is not composed of distinct and differential signifiers. The real is described as that which resists symbolization and signification, and is usually encountered in the context of trauma and psychosis. If, for instance, the NAME-OF-THE-FATHER cannot be integrated into the subject's symbolic world, the mechanism of FORECLOSURE [a specific psychical cause for psychosis] will ensure that it is expelled into the real and not repressed into the UNCONSCIOUS, thus triggering a PSYCHOSIS. (324)

Malkani finds it suitable to use realism, as much of it as is possible after what contemporary theories have made of it, (Morris 4) to describe this diseased kind of existence of the rudeboys. Realism is an apt tool for describing conditions that are not idealistic. To describe the sordid and the harsh conditions of life is to show the human lot as victims of their surroundings, some of which are of their own making. These unpleasant conditions bring people into conflicting situations that are needed and are vital in fiction. The essence of narrative and dramatic fiction lies in conflict. Pam Morris shows why realism is the right mode in this kind of fiction:

> Yet undeniably realism as a literary form has been associated with an insistence that art cannot turn away from the more sordid and harsh aspects of human existence. The stuff of realism is not selected for its dignity and nobility. More positively, realism participates in the democratic impulse of modernity. As a genre it has reached out to a much wider social range, in terms both of readership and of characters represented, than earlier more elite forms of literature. (3)

After some contemporary poststructuralist literary theories have demonstrated that meaning is fluid, even the meaning of realism is as fluid as anything else that claims potential truth. This chapter therefore examines realism to the extent that it can represent reality and truth convincingly and faithfully. The reality and truth in question is the reality and truth of the multicultural existence of the rudeboys in London. These rudeboys develop into people that their parents were not. They are a rebellious lot ready to break away from the bonding they may have had in their childhood with their parents. They can be seen as reflecting what Stuart Hall has said about youngsters settled in Western countries, youngsters who support Islamism. Chris Weedon describes Hall's view by suggesting that these youngsters would rather go to countries like Syria and Iraq to join hands with the jihadis, while women go there to marry them, rather than staying back in the Western countries to support the lifestyles of their parents. If Hall is a theorist of substance, so is Malkani as a novelist. Each of them points to the verisimilitude of the situation rather than to the truth.

It is the narrative voice that takes us into the heart of this novel. It is this which establishes the relationship between the narrator and the reader. This voice blends the two cultures: of the Brits, who are hardly seen except in Mr. Ashwood, but are always there somewhere in the background, and the Indians who have landed themselves in this foreign situation. This voice of Jas, the narrator, is the voice of the philosophy of multiculturalism. Jas is English but presented as Indian till the last but one chapter. He is one of the three main rudeboys; like them by choice but much softer inside. In him is multiculturalism as it ought to be, because he is both cultures in one man. The important thing about Jas is his façade; he is not as crude as he pretends to be. In a review of *Londonstani*, Pete L 'Official talks of this "expletive-adorned façade."

Jas is more sensitive and much more intellectual than the other rudeboys and yet he joins them. Perhaps he is attracted by their physical strength. We are told by him that he has got an A grade in his "GCSE History" course (133). A narrator in a novel must have a distinctive style and that is what Jas has in abundance. He narrates as one that has desires and needs like all normal beings but his physical strength and unaggressive makeup make him weak and uncertain. He allows himself to be dominated by women as well as men. His attempted affair with Samira turns out to be a damp one which makes him pitiable, and Sanjay bullies him into trying to steal his own father's warehouse. Through Jas, Malkani achieves, a union of opposites in the narrative style: the fusion of East and West, a feeble looking man and the support by the stronger rudeboys, an intelligent person doing things that would ruin him. His father is very disappointed in him, as any British parent would be, for getting into the mess of the Indian rudeboys and suffering without reason. He is very disappointed seeing that his English son wants to be identified as an Indian rudeboy:

—You say I don't know you. But you don't know me. All the time playing with those friends of yours. Remember how at one stage your mother and I even thought you were doing drugs because at least then your behaviour would make some sense. I ask you to come and watch football with me. You don't want it. What can I do?

—Dad, it's not that I don't want to, it's just—

—What? Because you think you're one of them?

—What?

—One of those Hardjit, Amit boys. You're not like them. We keep telling you. You don't want to know us because we keep telling you. What's wrong with us, son? What's wrong with us that you spend more time with Hardjit's father and mother than you do with your own father and mother? I know for a fact Hardjit's father never wants to watch football with his son. I know him. I know this. I know these things. Those two, father and son, they *really* don't know each other. But why do you pretend it's the same with us? And while Hardjit's father is always saying how his son abuses his Sikh religion, I've respected your ways, your youngster's version of Indian culture.... You're not like them, son. Now look at the trouble you're in. (339-40)

Malkani's stylistic technique and his thematic presentation of the multicultural philosophy of the novel cannot be said to be entirely original. But, as Pete L' Official points out, Malkani has put together something from Sam Selvon with another aspect of Irvine Welsh: "Thematically, the aimlessness and restlessness here recalls Sam Selvon's *The Lonely Londoners*, and stylistically, any comparisons to Irvine Welsh's *Trainspotting* are as inescapable as they are apt."

Jas's character shows that whereas once Indians wanted to be like the Brits and the Brits kept off Indians snobbishly, now it is the opposite or reverse. Jas's father wants him to be with the family and his other British connections but Jas would rather not be with his family and other British brethren; he is simply not interested in being with them. He would rather pretend to have an Indian identity. Malkani has shown, without ever saying so, that time changes and with it the power of nations. It is so ironical that the British Jas does not want to be considered British. He would rather be called a messy Indian rude-boy. Through the miracle of his narrator, Malkani has conveyed the current state of multiculturalism of the Indo-Brit situation in a most subtle manner.

Jas is the character we stay with all through the novel and he takes us through his journey of becoming an Indian. It seems that Malkani is suggesting that history has come full circle since Kamala Markandaya wrote, *The Nowhere Man* (1972-73), when Srinivas, an Indian had to do everything at the terms of the British and still be blamed and even killed by one of them. Now the situation is reversed. A young Briton is keen to imitate and be with the worst brand of Indians; those who neither have respect for their own nor Britain's culture. His parents have tried in vain to get him back to them. Between 1973 and 2006 multicultural relations have been completely changed. If this has not actually happened in Britain, then it could be the wishful thinking of an Indian author settled in England, one who has actually experienced what it is to live among the South Asians in Hounslow. It is quite evident that India has grown more, and faster, politically in the last two to three decades, than Britain. As a result, Indo-British equations have undergone some change. Some of this change is evident in the tone of Sir Vernon Ellis (Chairman of the British Council between 2010 and 2016):

> I was with Accenture for 40 years which has 70,000 people in India. I used to come to India quite a lot and I love it. I have also in recent years become much more involved with the arts as Chair of the English National Opera. One of the biggest hits of the ENO was Philip Glass' opera Satyagraha—which was in Sanskrit so nobody understood it!—but it did have a lot of cultural resonance! It's about Gandhi and South Africa and it's a very fine production. That interest in the arts was one of the reasons I was interested in this role. When I was here with David Cameron, he was then fresh in the job, it struck me that we have no right to a 'special relationship' with India. Here you are one of the big power houses of the world and Britain is a small island off the north coast of Europe with quite a history and some cultural assets but actually no right of place to be a prime partner in any way. If you look at the history of Britain and India there are many good things and not so many good

things and we have to do what is right for us together going forward. What he didn't mention much to begin with in his speeches was anything about Cultural Relations. He was very trade-focussed and one of the things I did with him on that trip, and so did Neil McGregor, was to emphasise that actually trade depends on trust between people and you build trust not just by saying "I'm a good partner" but by getting to know each other, understanding each other's needs and building a long-term relationship which is a trusted relationship. Actually even on that trip he began to use those words. William Hague, the foreign secretary, certainly understands it. He certainly understands that element of relations in the sense the British Council has a slightly different role and that the FCO has to take a self-interest, long term, mutuality, etc., but basically it's about British interests. I think we can take a more detached mutual interest.

An important question to be answered is, "Is Jas the voice of Gautam Malkani? Is he the character who carries the voice of the author?" The answer to this must be, yes, and no. Yes, because Jas is much like Malkani; living in England, a sort of hybrid existence. In a condition where it is difficult to say what the best course for this kind of hybrid existence should be. To be like the rudeboys is not dignified for Indians and to be like Brits is to be very unworthy. Jas is, in a sense, not like Malkani because he is, in the ultimate analysis, his own Other. Jas is a Brit trying to voice the feelings and situation of an Indian settled there.

II. The Language of *Londonstani*

F. R. Leavis's theory of the "exploratory creative use of language" can be rather profitably employed to set the basis for the language of *Londonstani*. In his essay, "Tragedy and the Medium," is to be found a sound theory of how the poet or novelist creates a language while exploring a subject that has to be presented through words. This kind of language whether used in poetry or prose is poetic and dramatic, as well as impersonal and religious (Bilan 103). A writer who employs this exploratory creative language uses it impersonally and with the depth and fervour that is found in religious experience. Jas's religious fervour comes due to the support of Hardjit and Ravi that he constantly gets. The word "religious" does not mean relating to a particular religion but rather relates to something treated or regarded with a devotion and scrupulousness appropriate to worship. Malkani's use of language may seem flawed, vulgar and even irritating, but it reflects the seriousness with which the novelist has absorbed the way people speak in "real life" strung by their egos and conscious minds. Malkani's characters are living, thinking and feeling entities that represent a certain section of people living in West London. The author is able to employ the language actually used by the men of Hounslow. If the language the people of this region use is coarse and ugly, the author uses this coarse and ugly language without trying to make it sound better than it is. According to Leavis, "the attainment in literature of this level, and of the organization of this level, would seem to involve the poetic use of language, or of processes that amount to that" (Bilan 103). By way of contrast Leavis explains that a mind tied to the use of such language will rise above its ego; "only the exploratory-creative use of language— coming from the depth of the self—allows the attainment of the level of experience at which the emancipation from the 'ready-defined self' is achieved" (Bilan 103). This kind of religious sense is to be found in the writings of D. H. Lawrence according to Leavis. Lawrence had invented a particular kind of language and style for communicating the experience of his time and place and Malkani has done that for his own time and place. *Londonstani* is a great novel because of a subtlety in its use of language. This language can be felt at two levels: First, it is used to paint the picture of vulgar and uncultured youngsters settled in West London. But more importantly it conveys the changing political position in which the Indian lot will not bend before the British to accept a continued state of colonization. Therefore, there is a deliberate attempt to use the English language in a rather uncouth, disrespectful and distorted form. The language shows defiance on the part of the Indians to which even the native British narrator has succumbed. All the politics of the novel can be said to lie in the vulgar use of the English language. The story begins with a distorted use of the English language to a large extent. The story is largely contained in the distortion of the English language (and this is an originality of its form). Rather than emerging only from its narrative, the story builds up from the way in which the youngsters use this language of rebellion. The subtlety of the use of language lies also in (i) balancing the shaky narration with a hybrid dialogue. (ii) The openness and forthrightness with which words are spoken and generally used in the novel. (iii) Maintaining originality in its use despite its vulgarity. Using totally new spellings throughout the novel and coining new words as some of the better-known British, American and other poets and prose writers have done. Various kinds of social groups use their own kinds of words and phrases. Jas's father for instance uses the phrase, "isn't it" like an Englishman would, not "innit" like the Indian rudeboys have been using it. Pete L' Official sums up the language of the novel and its narrator in the following words:

> An inner geek peeks from behind his [Jas's] expletive-adorned facade, sometimes charmingly so, as when Jas deigns to describe his nerdish youth: "I didn't get an E or a D in GCSE History, you see. I got me a muthafuckin A class, innit." His and his mates' vernacular, an anarchic swirl of slang, txt-msg talk, patois, Punjabi, Hindi, Urdu, and loads of "innits," crowds the book's first third, and it feels authentic to a point. Jas's jingle-jangle monologues don't convince, primarily because they are not so intended.

Here are some passages from the novel that reveal Malkani's unique, though artistically vulgarized use of language:

1. "—Serves him right he got his muthafuckin face fuck'd, shudn't b callin me a Paki, innit" (3). This is exactly the way the disgruntled South Asian youth, settled in West London, would speak. The frequent use of the word "fucking" and its variants in passages such as this takes away the sting of the word and makes it sound rather unabusive.

2. —Hear wat my bredren b sayin, sala kutta? Come out wid dat shit again n I'ma knock u so hard u'll b shittin out yo mouth 4 real, innit, goes Hardjit, with an eloquence an convention that made me green with envy. Amit always liked to point out that brown people don't actually go green:—we don't go red when we been shamed an we don't go blue when we dead, he'd said to me one time.—We don't even go purple when we been bruised, jus a darker brown. An still goras got da

front to call us coloured. (3)

This kind of language (the first part of this extract) makes it like an SMS message on a mobile phone or an internet message in general. The Hindi abusive words ("sala kutta") would endear some Indians and Pakistanis who use such language, having made it their own. The reference to brown people never going red, blue or purple, as the whites do, introduces the physiological difference between the races and hence marks out this group of people living in England as different to the natives.

> 3.—Fuckin ansa me, u dirty gora. Or is it dat yo glasses r so smash'd up u can't count? Shud've gone 2 Specsavers, innit. How many a us bredren b here?
> —F-F-F…
> For a second I thought the gora was gonna say something stupid. Something like F-F-Fuck off perhaps, or maybe even F-F-Fuck you. F-F-Fuckin Paki would've also been inadvisable. Stead he answers Hardjit with a straightforward,—F-F-Four.
> —Yeh, blud, safe, goes Ravi.—Gora ain't seein double, innit.
> So now it was Ravi's turn to make me jealous with his perfectly timed and perfectly authentic rudeboy front. I still use the word rudeboy cos it's been round for longer. People're always tryin to stick a label on our scene. That's the problem with havin a fuckin scene. First we was rudeboys, then we b Indian niggas, then rajamuffins, then raggastanis, Britasians, fuckin Indobrits. These days we try an use our own word for homeboy and so we just call ourselves desis but I still remember when we were happy with the word rudeboy. (5)

This extract reveals the violence that Indians face as residents of West London and how the rudeboys express their anxieties in a language that has become their language. What makes this language interesting is that in spite of the fact that the words used are not easy to understand, till one has got used to this language, with these words the author is able to do virtually everything that would be done with formal language; even make it sound humorous and living. The above extract also reveals how the rudeboys feel let down and frustrated in society; how a label is put on their group by people in a better position. There is great pain in the fact that they are "desis" living in a multicultural setup. There is always a consciousness of their being different and inferior as they are looked down upon rather than being looked up to.

4. All a this shit was just academic a course. Firstly, Hardjit's thesis, though it was what Mr Ashwood'd call internally coherent, failed to recognize the universality a the word Nigga compared with the word Paki. De-poncified, this means many Hindus and Sikh'd spit blood if they ever got linked to anything to do with Pakistan. Indians are just too racist to use the word Paki. Secondly, the white kid couldn't call no one a Paki no more with his mouth all cut up. It was still bleeding in little bursts, thick gobfuls droppin onto the concrete floor like he was slowly puking up blood or some shit. (7)

The above lines show the hatred which Indian youngsters have carried for people of Pakistan. How much bloody violence can erupt in a moment just because someone has called an Indian a Pakistani seems out of all proportion. Words such as "poncified" [blown out; adding a few pounds to your body] and "de-poncified" [collapsed; deflated; feeling as though some pounds were reduced in the body] belong to the vocabulary of this generation of youngsters settled in London. Such words can express more about these youngsters than more formal words can. The word "Nigga", which comes from the racist word, "Nigger" needs attention. These Indian youngsters and their theses have little value because their academic findings turn out to be less than universally acceptable. Hardjit's attempt to give to the word "Paki" the same connotation as the word "Nigger" fails to take off. The Indian youngsters are failures in the academic and in the Indo-Brit multicultural worlds. The only acceptance they sometimes get, we learn later in the novel, is from each other's parents; particularly mothers.

5. Amit'd always said goras couldn't ever get their facial hair right. If it weren't too blond, it was too curly or too bumfluffy or just too gimpy-shaped. One time he said that they looked like batty boys when they'd got facial hair an baby boys when they didn't. I told him I thought he was being racist. He goes to me it was the exact same thing as saying black guys were

good at growin dreadlocks but crap at growing ponytails. Amit probly had the wikedest facial hair in the whole a Hounslow, better than Hardjit's even. (8)

The above extract is significant for its tone and also because it is put in the mouth of a Brit character who has to speak about the less manly aspects of his people while he is seemingly Indian; it contains the defeatist complaining and grumbling of the Indian rudeboy, Amit, who out of irritation for, and annoyance with, the Brits makes fun of their comparatively less visible facial hair, calling them, "bumfluffy." This makes them less manly as facial hair is generally associated with manly strength. They are presented as "gimpy shaped", which is a way of saying that they look deformed and weak. As if that was not enough, they are also called "batty boys" which is the Jamaican term for homosexuals. In contrast, Amit looks manly due to his "wikedest facial hair in the whole a Hounslow". Hardjit too has this aspect in his personality. He too is Indian and manly.

III. The Dialogue

What makes *Londonstani* so different to other works of literary fiction is not only its language and style but also its unique kind of dialogue. Dialogue has been used so extensively in this novel that after a point, it seems to become the narrative itself. Half, or a little less than that, of the novel is in dialogue. This happens because whatever part of the novel is not in dialogue is the narrative of which Jas is the narrator. Jas, therefore, is an ever-present character in the novel, either speaking to others or telling us what is happening. Interestingly, the one who talks so much is the weakest of them all.

The dialogues of this novel have a distinctive feature; they are not in inverted commas. In fact Malkani has found a very original way of writing dialogue. He manages to blend them with the narrative by beginning a line in direct speech and, sometimes in the middle of the sentence, changing it into indirect speech. Here is an example:

—Ansa me, you dirty gora, Hardjit goes, before kneeling down an punching him in the mouth so that his tongue an lower lip explode again over the library books he'd tried to use as a shield. Even if the white kid could say something stead a just gurglin an splutterin blood, he was wise enough not to. (8)

There may be few or none who have blended direct and reported speech into the narrative as Malkani has done. What he achieves in such dialogues is a blending of showing and saying. His story goes on but a great many times without the narrator telling everything. The narrative takes on a more direct tone. In the above lines, for instance, we get a picture of how roughly Hardjit speaks in the first four words which are spoken by him. The rest of the lines are Jas's but we have already begun with the flavour of the roughness of Hardjit. Malkani has changed the usual name, "Harjeet" to "Hardjit" perhaps trying to show the hardness of his character. That is how the British, Jas, would pronounce it, retaining the advantage of the connotation of "hard" in his name. In Jas's dialogues are some very fine coinages of words that only a genius of linguistic abilities like Malkani could have made. His coinage of the word, "jackshit" for instance is remarkable (298). The word, "jack" has been clubbed with some other words like "knife", "fruit", "ass", "boot", etc. making them "jack-knife", "jackfruit", "jackass" and "jackboot", respectively. It should be noted that the poet Gerard Manley Hopkins had similarly coined the word, "Jackself" in his sonnet, "My Own Heart."

The strength of *Londonstani* lies in the manner of its narration, its use of language and the new kind of dialogue Malkani has invented. The plot of the novel is hardly noticeable. Very little happens in the novel except the fact that the rudeboys have been stealing mobile phone-handsets of people to reprogram them and sell them. They make the mistake of stealing the handset of their school teacher, Mr Ashwood. As a result, his former pupil, Sanjay, who seems to be helping the rudeboys, actually corners Jas and forces him to steal from his own father's warehouse. A fire breaks out in the warehouse; Jas is kicked, bounced around like a basketball and beaten. He has to be hospitalized. It is in the hospital we meet his parents and get to know that he is British. The great merit of the novel is that it shows us a totally new face of multiculturalism, one in which Indians of this category paint a poor picture of themselves but nevertheless seem to impress a few Britons.

Malkani puts in the issue of multiculturalism rather subtly into *Londonstani*. That is the advantage in saying things in fiction, where the method is to show it, or merely suggest it, rather than stating it blatantly. Multiculturalism in contemporary terminology is the co-existence of different cultures in a geographical space that leads either to conflicts or a conscious effort to tolerate the other in a civilized manner. It is a geo-political phenomenon. There are mental adjustments no doubt, but whether there is an actual amalgamation of culturally different people is what matters. Fiction has always come forward to reflect this problem and to reflect upon it. Even since the world of the ancient Greeks there has been cultural diversity, people sharing different religions, languages and culture came into Greece from Aetolia, Locris, Doris and Epirus. In the Ottoman Empire, there were Christians, Jews, pagan Arabs, and other religious groups in a geographical space where Muslims formed the majority. The human lot has been learning how to suffer each other with the advancement of time. With this happening, pretensions of a happy co-existence are made. *Londonstani* has shown the extent to which two races suffer each other without actually colliding against each other. Violence is more in the language used within groups that can be called "closed societies" than in actions that settlers from places like India indulge in as they live in London. Yet there are feelings of hatred brewing within those groups of people and any reader of *Londonstani* will notice this ill will towards each other.

Malkani brings up the difference between bigotry and racism. The British couple, Jas's parents, is the one to talk about the difference when Jas is admitted in hospital after being injured. Jas's father believes that he and his wife have been much superior in their relationship with their son than have been the parents of Jas's friend, Hardjit. He believes that they know their son much better and have been much closer emotionally to him than Hardjit's parents have been to their son. Jas's father is piqued that, "Those two, father and son, they really don't know each other. But why do you pretend it's the same with us? And while Hardjit's father is always saying how his son abuses his Sikh religion, I've respected your ways, your youngster's version of Indian culture" (340). He claims that he and Jas's mother have tried to be friends with Hardjit's family for his sake. His mother has even tried to cook like their mothers. He then insists that Jas is not like his Indian friends:

—What're you tryin to say, Dad? Mum, what's Dad tryin to say?
—You know exactly what your father's saying, Jas.

—Yes. You know exactly what I'm saying, Jas. You think I'm being… what's that fancy word you always use? A bigot? You think I don't want you to hang around with these other boys because I'm a bigot? Why can't you just use the word racist, Jas? That's what you think, isn't it? That your mother and I are racist? Isn't that what you think, Jas? I don't even know why we agree to use this Jas nonsense nickname of yours anyway, I mean what kind of a name is that, Jason? You hear what your mother and I are trying to say to you, Jason?

I didn't even look at him.

—What nonsense is this? You don't even respond to your own name? Jason Bartholomew-Cliveden, do you hear what I'm saying?

Then Dad grabs the clipboard from the end a my bed an, like, shoves it in my face.—Look, he says.—It says your name here on your medical chart: Jason Bartholomew-Cliveden, aged nineteen, white, male. (340)

Works Cited

Barnes, Julian, *The Sense of an Ending*. Vintage Books, 2012.

Bell, James Scott. *Voice: The Secret Power of Great Writing*. Compendium Press, 2015.

Bilan, R. P. *The Literary Criticism of F. R. Leavis*. Cambridge UP, 1979.

Cobley, Paul. *Narrative. The New Critical Idiom*. Routledge, 2013.

Edgerton, Les. *Finding Your Voice*. Blue Skies Books, 2012.

Ellis, Sir Vernon. "Cultural Relations in the Twenty-first Century—India-UK". 11 May 2011, https://www.britishcouncil.in/sites/default/files/cultural_relations_roundtable_delhi_trancript-may_2012.pdf.

Graham, James. "'This isn't Good Will Hunting': *Londonstani* and the market for London's multicultural fictions" *Literary London: Interdisciplinary Studies in the Representation of London*, vol 6, issue 2, September 2008.

———. "An Interview with Gautam Malkani: Ealing Broadway, 6th November 2007." *Literary London: Interdisciplinary Studies in the Representation of London*, vol 6, issue 1, March 2008, http://www.literarylondon.org/london-journal/march2008/graham.html.

Lodge, David. *The Language of Fiction*. Routledge, 2012.

Macey, David. *The Penguin Dictionary of Critical Theory*. Penguin Books, 2001.

Malkani, Gautam. "A Coversation with Gautam Malknai" *Londonstani* Reader's Guide http://www.penguinrandomhouse.com/books/298988/londonstani-by-gautam-malkani/9780143112280/readers-guide/).

McLaren, Peter. "White Terror and Oppositional Agency: Towards a Critical Multiculturalism." *Multiculturalism: A Critical Reader*. Edited by David Goldberg, Blackwell Publishers Ltd, 1995, pp. 45-74.

Morris, Pam. *Realism. The New Critical Idiom*. Routledge, 2009.

Official, Pete L'. "A Review of Londonstani by Gautam Malkani". August 2006, https://www.believermag.com/issues/200608/?read=review_malkani.

Rosoff, Meg. *The Guardian*, Tuesday 18 October 2011. https://www.theguardian.com/books/2011/oct/18/how-to-write-fiction-meg-rosoff.

Weedon, Chris. "Stuart Hall, the British multicultural question and the case of western jihadi brides." *International Journal of Cultural Studies*, vol. 19, issue 1, 2016, pp. 101-16.

CHAPTER SIX

Culture, Language and the Post-Truth World

When people chose democracy over more autocratic forms of government, the reason was that they wanted everyone to get at least some basic rights. This was possible only through an organized, orderly existence which needed a basic minimum of civilization, culture and socialization. The consciousness of these entailed some basic tenets of rights and duties that were to be understood and communicated through language. Whether one spoke the truth or the lie, one had to do that through language. Contemporary literary theories tell us that we cannot and, indeed, never speak the whole truth. Yet democratic and civilized behaviour demands that we try to speak the truth for the sake of the convenience of all. So, truth ultimately is not natural to most of us. It does not come as naturally as leaves come to a tree, and yet we make an effort to keep close to it. But in the evolutionary advancement, we have moved from savagery to civilization and now we seem to be moving in the opposite direction. We seem to be going towards a political and social scenario in which trying to seem very civilized and cultured is neither essential nor possible and it is a state that does not consider truth to be a necessary part of our existence. Yet we live in an age flooded with news. We must keep receiving this news, even at the cost of it becoming fake news.

This article is an attempt to show that culture, with some of its related aspects such as education and religion, has directly impacted the lives of democratic societies and this impact is reflected in the language people use. In the post-truth scenario this relationship between culture and language has become evident in a different way because truth is becoming the scapegoat. The desire to be truthful has been supplanted by the desire to seem impressive. Politics is based largely on falsehoods. Truth no longer attracts as it did for say, a Gandhian in India or an English-speaking Westerner brought up to respect the spill-over of Arnoldian humanism. This has happened both in the West and in the East. This is what d 'Ancona has to say in this regard:

> We have entered a new phase of political and intellectual combat in which democratic orthodoxies and institutions are being shaken to their foundations by a wave of ugly populism. Rationality is threatened by emotion, diversity by nativism, liberty by a drift towards autocracy. More than ever, the practice of politics is perceived as a zero-sum game, rather than a contest between ideas.... At the heart of this global trend is a crash in the value of truth, comparable to the collapse of a currency or a stock. Honesty and and accuracy are no longer assigned the highest priority in political exchange.... 69 % of Trump's statements are "Mostly False", "False" or "Pants on Fire."

Similarly, in the UK, the campaign to leave the European Union won with slogans that were untrue or misleading.

Whenever there are too many sinners the Hindu God is born in a new avatar. And whenever there is confusion in literary matters a critic emerges to take account of the situation. In the world of post-truth too, the literary critic should play a more significant role. It is time he came out of the literature closet and addressed the democratic world. For literature is related to life, and life, now, definitely needs the critic's intervention.

Matthew Arnold had looked upon language in a unique manner. He admired the French for the way they had mastered and used their language. He believed that language and the divine are, or were, connected in a unique way. David G Riede's *Matthew Arnold and the Betrayal of Language* (2015) begins with the premise that the disappearance or death of God in the nineteenth century meant also the death of the Logos. [Logos may be defined as "reason or the rational principle expressed in words and things, argument, or justification; especially personified as the source of order in the universe."] Riede maintains that like the speaker in the "Stanza from the Grand Chartreuse" Arnold was caught between two worlds: The first was a past in which "language had created only what proved to be the emptiness of shattered creeds," and the other "a future for which an adequate vocabulary had yet not evolved." Arnold was a poet and agnostic torn apart between these conflicting demands. Whereas on the one hand he denied the talismanic power of language but required a voice more authoritative than that of the subject self, on the other he regarded the the language of science as above truthful but nevertheless sterile. Out of the tensions produced by this conflict, Reide maintains came poems of special interest to the postmodernist critic. Why did this cultural critic pay so much attention to language? The reason was twofold: First, language had the power to put across the "idea", which to Arnold was the basic constituent of poetry. Second, language was an essential part of culture. It was through language and poetry that culture could be preserved and anarchy could be avoided.

Matthew Arnold was one of the nineteenth century's greatest spokesmen for the saving power of culture, especially of poetry, to substitute for a vanishing religion. Yet he was persistently troubled throughout his career by the difficulty of finding adequate authority in language. *Matthew Arnold and the Betrayal of Language* explores Arnold's attempts to find an authoritative language, and argues that his occasional claims for such a language reveal more uneasiness than confidence in the value of "letters."

Arnold could say that the idea was what poetry contained (something that was conveyed through language), science contained facts which were different to ideas and less enduring. Hence the future of poetry was immense; it had the potential to play the role of religion and hence contained some kind of truth. Literature therefore can substitute religion as the bearer of truth. For Arnold there was a direct connection between morality, religion, culture, language and truth.

F. R. Leavis was one of those modernists who relied very heavily on some of Arnold's principles. He too was a moralist, supporter of the affirmative principle of literature, and expected literature to support life. He too was a cultural critic and had a clear idea of what role universities should play. In writing *The Living Principle* Leavis's purpose was one that is rarely attempted by critics. To justify the claim that literary studies in general, literary criticism in particular, and indeed the whole practice and institution of literature, are worthwhile human enterprises. Leavis considered literature as a body of ideas rather than an implicit force of driving impulse underlying the dedication to practical criticism of a powerful and human thinker. In Leavis's theory, Hugh Bredin tells us, there is nothing as important as language; his views on language are the most central part to the justification of literature. Bredin further says that Leavis's theory rests upon a conception of the

mind often associated with Locke. According to this view, thought de-
rives from impressions passively received through the medium of the
senses. It is easy to see how much language and culture are connected.
Literature is made of ideas, ideas are made of language, language comes
from impressions passively received but it leads to culture. Literature
must be true to life and in a language that is exploratory-creative if it
is to be great. Truth is therefore dependent on a language that is found
suitable to the subject being dealt with in literature.

Raymond Williams, however, has shown how changes in language
have been changing culture; culture itself is hardly regarded as an embodiment of the perfection that was sought by elitist societies through
it. Williams points this out in his book *Culture and Society*:

> …it is possible to look again at those wider changes in life and
> thought to which the changes in language evidently refer. Five
> words are the key points from which this map can be drawn.
> They are industry, democracy, class, art and culture. The im-
> portance of these words, in our modern structure of meanings,
> is obvious. The changes in their use, at this critical period, bear
> witness to a general change in our characteristic ways of think-
> ing about our common life: about our social, political and eco-
> nomic institutions; about the purposes which these institutions
> are designed to embody; and about the relations to these insti-
> tutions and purposes of our activities in learning, education
> and the arts.

Williams further points out the two meanings of culture and considers culture to be ordinary:

> Culture is ordinary: that is the first fact. Every human society
> has its own shape, its own purposes, and its own meanings.
> Every human society expresses these, in institutions, and in
> arts and learning. The making of a society is the finding of
> common meanings and directions, and its growth is an active
> debate and amendment under the pressures of experience, con-
> tact, and discovery, writing themselves into the land…. Then,
> second, but equal in importance, is the testing of these in ex-
> perience, the making of new observations, comparisons, and
> meanings…. We use the word culture in these two senses: to

mean a whole way of life—the common meanings; to mean the arts and learning—the special processes of discovery and creative effort. Some writers reserve the word for one or other of these senses; I insist on both, and on the significance of their conjunction. The questions I ask about our culture are questions about deep personal meanings. Culture is ordinary, in every society and in every mind.

It is quite clear that language which is made of words is changing because the meaning of words is changing, as Williams has shown. Even what we understand by the term "culture" is changing. The changing nature of language is creating complications of the difference between fact and fiction.

But since Raymond Williams stipulated his position, much has changed. Language in the post-truth world has tended more and more to obscure the difference between fact and fiction. As a result, democracy is in danger. For a successful democracy it is vitally necessary to have a sound education and this education needs a rich, mature and an evolved language. Culture demands a disciplined commitment to language. The role of literature and the humanities can hardly be over-emphasized in the building up of such cultured societies. But the world of post-truth, as captured in literary texts, and even outside them, is one that has given up the quest for cultural and linguistic advancement. In such a situation truth takes the backseat and emotional or theatrical lies that impress become the order of the day.

The literary critic, then, has been the best arbiter in matters of language, literature, culture and education. In the post-truth world, too, the literary critic can come up with great suggestions regarding how to cope with this fake-news situation. I therefore turn to the critic, Christopher Schaberg, to see what he makes of the post-truth situation. In his book *The Work of Literature in the Age of Post-Truth* (July 2018), he comes up with some very relevant observations. He comes up with the theory that the domain of literature is a space where readers "linger in and learn from uncertainty, ambiguity and paradox." One who tries to delve deep into the "Truth" with a capital "T" is likely to be using Truth in the service of some interest or power. Schaberg maintains:

Careful study of rhetoric and context often reveals claims of Truth to be riddled with contradiction or indeterminacy. So getting to a place of post-truth may have sounded like a worthwhile venture, not so long ago.

But post-truth means something more sinister these days.... This is the age when what is truthfully stated or factually reported can be dismissed as "just words"—as Donald Trump put it in his first debate with Hillary Clinton. And by merely retorting that something is not true, any further inquiry is halted.

It is necessary to remember "the slippery nature of truth" that Nietzsche pointed to and to take his advice and turn to perspectivism. And then we will look at life as we should be looking at literature, like critics, and its various perspectives. Believers in perspectivism say that all ideations take place from particular perspectives, and that there are many possible conceptual schemes, or perspectives in which judgment of truth or value can be made. Works of literature also can be seen through various perspectives as they open up the gates of interpretation with no firm foundations to fall back on. Literature is what is needed in this troubled post-truth time. Language, as it is used today in politics and other matters, should not be taken to mean something final. It should be taken in the spirit that literature is taken by the literary critic.

We have seen how meaning has become more and more fluid in the post-Matthew Arnold era. Critics like Leavis and Williams have shown how every succeeding phase is a step away from what language did or what "truth" meant. The literary critic is then the one who can best handle the slipperiness of truth in the post-truth era. It is he who must be relied upon to tell the world about the import of the utterances of politicians and other important tellers of weaponized lies. If literary statements have multilayered meanings, non-literary statements too can have that dimension. The critic must stand between the teller and the listener to make the situation less grim.

Works Cited

Bredin, Hugh. *Critical Quarterly*, June 1982.

Leavis, F. R. *The Living Principle*. Ivan R. Dee; 1st Elephant pbk. edition (1998).

Riede, David G. *Matthew Arnold and the Betrayal of Language*. University of Virginia Press (2015).

Schaberg, Christopher. *The Work of Literature in the Age of Post-Truth* Bloomsbury Academic, (2018).

Williams, Raymond. *Culture and Society: 1780-1950*. Columbia University Press; 2nd ed. (1983).

———. "Culture is Ordinary" http://artsites.ucsc.edu/faculty/gustafson/film%20162.w10/readings/williams.ordinary.pdf.

CHAPTER SEVEN

The Biographical and Autobiographical:
Two Canadian Poems

A biographical poem is not necessarily about the person it claims to portray. It can equally be about the poet writing it to a rather large extent. An autobiographical poem is selective and will often conceal much and reveal only some aspects of the author. When you read a biographical poem such as Margaret Atwood's "Disembarking at Quebec," followed by an autobiographical one like Michael Ondaatje's "Letters & Other Worlds" it becomes clear that though the two are both Canadian they have almost nothing in common except an indication that multiculturalism is difficult to carry through with perfect success and that cultural difference is difficult to wipe out. The two poets are, in the poems in this article, somewhat antipodal at least on some grounds. Ondaatje projects the suffering of a man whose family did not support him early on, while Atwood almost never allows the speaker in the poem, Susanna Moodie, to suffer as seriously as the male in Ondaatje's poem does. At best the persona in Atwood's poem feels a little alienated. Ondaatje's poem seems to voice an Asian male's calm acceptance whereas Atwood's poem contains a Western woman's unyielding attitude. It is in autobiographical poems, it seems, that readers can get a truer picture of the poet at a certain point of time. The biographical poem takes you to the poet indirectly; it shows a poet finding points of compatibility or incompatibility in another, for the poet notices things that she shares with others or finds unfamiliar in them. Even as a persona is found to speak out the lines of Atwood's poem, she voices the feelings of the poet. The two poems that I am examining, Ondaatje's "Letters & Other Worlds" and Atwood's "Disembarking at Quebec," have been chosen because each is Canadian and each has something of a person unsettled by intercultural mixing. While these poems are extremely dissimilar in form and content, each gives a glimpse of the poet writing and points to the kind of consciousness that informs it. Atwood often writes to voice the suffering of women as she does in *The Handmaid's Tale* (1985); Ondaatje sometimes ends up showcasing the pains men go through. *The English Patient* (1992) for instance has been considered a novel that brings to the reader the problem of male depression.

At a time when we have already travelled through and beyond formalistic readings of poems, a situation in which the poem lives while the poet is virtually nonexistent, this article can be meaningful because it points to the fact that in a poem, particularly, of an autobiographical nature, the poet is hardly dead. In a poem where the poet writes of another instead of the self, she is still present in some measure. It is true that the autobiographical part of the poem may not always be an entirely realistic representation of the poet, but it still is some representation.

"Disembarking at Quebec" figures in one of Atwood's best poetry collections, *The Journals of Susanna Moodie* (1970). The speaker in this poem is Susanna Moodie, the nineteenth century English-born Canadian writer who dwelt upon her experiences as a settler in Canada, then a British colony. This poem is the very first in the collection and its position in Atwood's collection is significant. Through this positioning she says certain things. For instance, she shares with the reader the centrality of women in her scheme of things; she shows a woman emigrating in Canada. This free verse poem provides the setting of the travels of Susanna Moodie. The woman is looking for a better life after leaving home. Home is a central issue with feminist writers and this poem is therefore very significant for a feminist poet like Atwood.

According to William Herbert New, the reader of "Disembarking in Quebec" must know that the woman in this poem is not so much a historical person who emerges from Moodie's own letters as she is an icon of cultural schizophrenia, "a symbol of what it is to be female in Canada in 1970" (243). Atwood transforms a nineteenth century author into a twentieth century immigrant. The poem is not one with feminist concern alone. It has postcolonial perspective and a feeling of whether multicultural life, a happy coexistence, will be possible in Quebec for the woman in the poem. It is necessary to quote the poem to show the sensitivity of the poet which blends all these issues into a near perfect whole:

Is it my clothes, my way of walking,
the things I carry in my hand
—a book, a bag with knitting-
the incongruous pink of my shawl

this space cannot hear

or is it my own lack
of conviction which makes
these vistas of desolation,
long hills, the swamps, the barren sand, the glare
of sun on the bone-white
driftlogs, omens of winter,
the moon alien in day-
time a thin refusal

The others leap, shout

Freedom!

The moving water will not show me
my reflection.

The rocks ignore.

I am a word
in a foreign language.

Atwood creates the picture of a woman walking into an alien land, feeling like an "Other", in a nineteenth century colonial situation. She cannot identify with the place and seems to be reduced to "a word in a foreign language." There is a fine crafting of the natural world and the human situation juxtaposed each with the other. In the foreign land, even the rocks seem to ignore the lady, and the moving water will not show her reflection. Even the nature of the place has left her alone and alienated.

Alongside this alienating process there is another factor that has been pointed out by Colin Nicholson. In the bordering United States can be seen a contrast to the situation in which the European woman finds herself in her new existence:

> A specifically European identity struggles towards Canadian recognition and self-recognition in ways that foreground both the confusions of immigrant consciousness and the indeterminacies generated by conflict between inherited and indigenous code of perception. 'This space cannot hear', cries the woman in the opening poem of the collection, as middle-class sensibility comes into contact with an unprepossessing and alien Quebecois Other, and envy for contemporary optimism south of the border in the United States is registered: 'The others leap, shout/ Freedom!' (38)

This poem points towards an impending failure of multiculturalism in Canada and Europe, a theme that Michael Ondaatje also takes up in *The English Patient*. Further, it indicates the failure of women to blend into multicultural societies. In multicultural societies, it is the women that are more marginalized. The woman walking alone complains that the "space" of Canada cannot "hear" her walk, her feminine presence—her clothes, the way in which she walks, the things she carries like a book, a bag and knitting, the particular shade of pink in her shawl from back home—will mean very little to the alien society.

Atwood's poem has then, through the persona of a nineteenth century immigrant woman expresses concerns that are dear to her own sensibility. Even as she describes Susanna Moodie, her poem picks up issues that are present in most of her own literary works. Feminist and postcolonial perspectives enter her text. The fact that she herself kept coming in and out of Quebec in her childhood cannot be missed out. The biography one writes can indeed have connections with one's own life.

The second poem in this article, Ondaatje's "Letters and Other Worlds," is autobiographical. Yet it has some links with the first because in it again the poet is talking about another, his father, and in doing that is talking about himself to an extent. For what we notice in another has some connections with our own world and point of view. But in comparative terms it is of a much more personal nature because it mentions the suffering of the poet's own father:

My father's body was a globe of fear
His body was a town we never knew
He hid that he had been where we were going
His letters were a room he seldom lived in

Ondaatje seems to recollect the fear his father had as he lived, trapped in a bad marriage. Geographical images abound in the early part of the poem; they describe the neurosis and the uneasy life of the poet's father, Mervyn Ondaatje, who separated from his wife, Doris Gratiaen, after having struggled in a family strife. His parents divorced each other several times. He took to drinking heavily and wrote perhaps to escape his neurosis. This poem being autobiographical, it would help to see the circumstances in the author's life that led to it. Born in Kegalle, Sri Lanka on 12 September 1943, Michael Ondaatje did not feel exactly at home in this country because his ancestors were of European origin (Dutch) and they came to Sri Lanka between the sixteenth and seventeenth centuries. For him life in Sri Lanka, then called Ceylon, was something of a colonial experience, living amidst a people who didn't exactly belong to his homeland. His father, Mervyn Ondaatje, was not very well adjusted in this country and took to heavy drinking perhaps because of his relationship with his wife and his inability to mingle well with another culture. On the whole Michael Ondaatje considered himself belonging to the east because of his father and with links to the West because of his mother.

Mervyn Ondaatje's fierce nostalgia for the manners and mores of this neo-colonial Ceylonese social caste was a continuing presence throughout Ondaatje's childhood years. These childhood years were darkened by the spectre of Mervyn Ondaatje's chronic alcoholism (Spinks 1). Mervyn and Doris Ondaatje were divorced in 1945 when the author was just two. Doris Ondaatje, left for England in 1948. Michael and his sister lived with their relatives in Colombo away from their father, who was in Kegalle. Michael Ondaatje went to his mother in England later, when he was nine in 1952. He had earlier stayed back in Sri Lanka because he was two when his mother left for England. During this early age in life, he had to depend on his own emotional resources. At age nine, he went to England and spent ten unhappy years staying with his elder brother in London and getting schooled there till such time as he was old enough to get enrolled as a major in English and History at Bishops University, Lennoxville, in Quebec, Canada.

He had considered himself part of the South-East Asia diaspora in London. It was in Canada that he began to feel at ease. He became aware of the writings of several Canadian authors such as Daphne Marlatt, BP Nichol, Raymond Souster, Dennis Lee, Al Purdy, Margaret Avison and Nicole Brossard; and then in the years that followed, the appearance of writers like Margaret Atwood, Alice Munro, Margaret Laurence and Robert Kroetsch gave him a feel of who he was as a writer. When he wrote *The English Patient* he had already spent thirty years in Canada. By now he had experienced three different cultures—the Sri Lankan, the English and the Canadian—and apart from these he had inherited, genetically, the culture of the Holland from which his ancestors hailed.

It may be said of Ondaatje that first as a colonizer he was part of one diaspora in Sri Lanka. Then as one born in Sri Lanka he became a migrant to the UK and finally a migrant as well as resident of Canada. There could be few individuals with such multicultural experience as Ondaatje had. He could indeed be considered one without the sense of belonging to a distinct culture or a place. "Letters & Other Worlds" was written after Mervyn Ondaatje had died. It is a very sad poem because it contains the love of the poet for his father, a love that he could never share. He hardly had much contact with his father except through the letters that his father wrote to him and the letters the poet wrote in reply to his father. The other contact that the poet had with his father was through the writings of his father, something that his father had kept hidden from his family.

The poem, like a true autobiographical account, tells the reader that while the father lived in fear, his sons and family didn't quite know the condition in which the father lived. They had few meeting points and therefore remained ignorant. In contrast to the above, the father constructed another world for himself, the world of the letters, mainly his writings, but this world of letters scarcely kept him within it. The father's letters could be like a room he very rarely lived in in his actual life. But these letters or writings are a space where "the logic of his love could grow." The "logic of his love" is an unusual phrase. It is, however, one that indicates that his father had a kind of love, a love that did not find fulfillment. He therefore wrote as a poet writes but lived unlike most poets in drunkenness. Whereas most poets are able to counter their neurosis through writing, this man did not do that but tried to counter it through drinking. His body therefore remained a "town of fear." He tried to hide himself from his writings so that his family may not discover him in them to realize how terrified and anxious he was. Furthermore, the terrible picture of the man that emerged from his writings even scared him to death—"He came to death with his mind drowning." He drank two bottles of gin in a closed room and fell down dying when his blood vessels burst and blood spread elsewhere in a hemorrhage.

The poet describes his father's early life as a "terrifying comedy." His mother was divorcing his father again and again. The picture of the man is rather clear. Imagine the plight of a man whose wife invites him to her again and again only to divorce him. The comedy is to be seen in the actions that the father who leaves her, gets drunk, goes into train-tunnels and becomes famous for the wrong things. He once stopped a whole procession of elephant dancers, local dignitaries in Sri Lanka, by falling dead dunk onto a street. This procession is known locally as "Perahara." This act made a little impact on Sri Lanka's gaining home rule in 1948.

The mother was no bundle of virtues. She drove her car wildly. As a result it was often stoned by villagers. Both parents claimed that he or she was "the injured party." His mother would sometimes defend her husband's faults but only to an extent. She, for instance, said that he was drunk rather than broken hearted when he behaved oddly in company. He ultimately started staying in closed rooms where he composed his apologies, speeches and his other writings. His new wife's arrival made little difference to his mental agonies. He could write with clarity no doubt but never get healed through his writing. His tragic fall left his mind without a metaphor because it suffered the terrible hemorrhage.

The poem becomes much more interesting after one reads Michael Ondaatje's memoir, *Running in the Family*, where we learn of the kind of father the poet had. Mervyn Ondaatje, in his young days, had enough problems to suit almost anyone. His stay at Cambridge where he did everything but study and then disarm his family by pretending to be engaged to Kaye Roseleaps, returning to Sri Lanka and then before the engagement shocking his family by announcing his engagement to Doris Gratiaen. Such was the stuff that the young Mervyn Ondaatje was made of. He remained unaffected by the hornets he stirred up in his family. The dying father who suffers in the poem is one who seems to have invited his problems with a reckless life:

Two weeks after he arrived in Ceylon, my father came home one evening to announce that he was engaged to a Doris Gratiaen. The postponed argument at Cambridge now erupted on my grandfather's lawn in Kegalle. My father was calm and unconcerned with the various complications he seemed to have created and did not even plan to write to the Roseleaps. (*Running in the Family* 19)

Ondaatje writes of the sufferings of his father but as he does that we feel that the poem describes his own suffering because he is the sensitive son of the suffering father. Ondaatje could have found in this suffering, traces that his own life was going through; there is perhaps some self-identification of the son with the father. He too married twice, the first wife was Kim Jones and the second is the Canadian novelist, Linda Spalding, and it is a matter of biographical research to find out the impact his first marriage had on his life.

Ondaatje's nickname was Kip and that is the name he gave to the Indian sapper, Kripal Singh in *The English Patient*. His sympathies are with his father rather than mother and therefore he seems to be rather concerned with the suffering male. Kip suffers and Mervyn Ondaatje suffers; and Michael Ondaatje suffers in his consciousness through them. The autobiographical poem takes us directly to the suffering of the suffering father's son; Atwood's biographical poem takes us indirectly to the empathy of the poet for the suffering woman. The man in Ondaatje's poem is able to speak out his suffering a little more clearly than the woman in Atwood's poem. Does this indicate that women are changing in the contemporary world, trying to keep back their feelings, even as men are going ahead with a more candid expression of them?

Works Cited

Atwood, Margaret. *The Journals of Susanna Moodie*. OUP Canada, 1970.

Gilligan, Carol. "The Hollow Men: A therapist examines the hidden problem of male depression" https://archive.nytimes.com/www.nytimes.com/books/97/02/16/reviews/970216.16gilligt.html.

New, William Herbert. *A History of Canadian Literature*. McGill-Queen's Press, 2003.

Nicholson, Colin. *Margaret Atwood: Writing and Subjectivity: New Critical Essays*. Palgrave Macmillan UK, 1994.

Ondaatje, Michael. *The Cinnamon Peer: Selected Poems*. Knopf 1991.

———. *Running in the Family*. Bloomsbury, 2016.

Spinks, Lee. *Michael Onddatje* Contemporary World Writers. Manchester University Press, 2009.

OTHER ANAPHORA LITERARY PRESS TITLES

The History of British and
American Author-Publishers
By: Anna Faktorovich

Notes for Further Research
By: Molly Kirschner

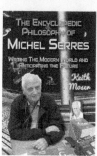

The Encyclopedic Philosophy of
Michel Serres
By: Keith Moser

The Visit
By: Michael G. Casey

How to Be Happy
By: C. J. Jos

A Dying Breed
By: Scott Duff

Love in the Cretaceous
By: Howard W. Robertson

The Second of Seven
By: Jeremie Guy

CPSIA information can be obtained
at www.ICGtesting.com
Printed in the USA
LVHW042344300919
632726LV00003B/194/P